The Romance of Wealth - Personal Finance for Couples

Practical Tips to Stop Fighting About Money, Relieve Financial Stress, Increase Savings, and Make Your Relationship Thrive

Jackie L. Pierce

© **Copyright 2023 - All rights reserved.**

The content contained within this book may not be reproduced, duplicated or transmitted without direct written permission from the author or the publisher.

Under no circumstances will any blame or legal responsibility be held against the publisher, or author, for any damages, reparation, or monetary loss due to the information contained within this book, either directly or indirectly.

Legal Notice:

This book is copyright protected. It is only for personal use. You cannot amend, distribute, sell, use, quote or paraphrase any part, or the content within this book, without the consent of the author or publisher.

Disclaimer Notice:

Please note the information contained within this document is for educational and entertainment purposes only. All effort has been executed to present accurate, up to date, reliable, complete information. No warranties of any kind are declared or implied. Readers acknowledge that the author is not engaged in the rendering of legal, financial, medical or professional advice. The content within this book has been derived from various sources. Please consult a licensed professional before attempting any techniques outlined in this book.

By reading this document, the reader agrees that under no circumstances is the author responsible for any losses, direct or indirect, that are incurred as a result of the use of the information contained within this document, including, but not limited to, errors, omissions, or inaccuracies.

Contents

Introduction — 1

Arjun's Story — 5

1. Money Talk: Exploring Your Emotional Relationship with Wealth — 6
   Money Scripts: Understanding the Common Internal Narratives that Drive Financial Behavior and Decision-Making
   The Role of Upbringing and Culture in Shaping Our Money Mindset
   Activity: Money Mindset Quiz for Couples

Ella's Story — 17

2. The Financial Heartstrings: How Money Affects Your Emotions — 18
   The Interplay of Fear, Guilt, and Shame: Unraveling Their Impact on Financial Decision-Making
   Navigating Financial Differences: Common Conflicts in Couples with Differing Values, Goals, and Priorities

Nora and Ben's Story — 34

3. Financially in Sync: How to Align Your Money Values and Goals Together — 36
   Breaking Down Personal Barriers to Financial Partnership
   Three Essential Financial Discussions for You and Your Partner
   Five Simple Steps to Get on the Same Page Financially

    Providing Strategies for Addressing and Overcoming Financial Fears in a Partnership

Maria and Jack's Story   55

4. Communication About Money: How to Talk About Money Without Fighting or Shaming   57
   Fostering Financial Harmony Through Understanding Perspectives
   Active Listening: A Key to Understanding

Samantha and Alex's Story   67

5. United We Stand: Aligning Your Financial Priorities   69
   Section 1: Investment Styles and Strategies
   Section 2: Setting Joint Investment Goals
   Section 3: Retirement Goals and Saving Strategies
   Section 4: Planning for Your Children's Educational Future
   Section 5: Managing Debt as a Couple

Ted and Marcus's Story   103

6. Two Hearts, One Wallet: Fostering Shared Dreams and Passion   105
   Managing and Prioritizing Multiple Financial Goals
   Harnessing the Power of Visualization as a Couple to Transform Your Money Mindset

Maya and Leo's Story   119

7. Teamwork Makes the Dream Work: Structuring Monthly Finances and Division of Responsibilities   120
   The Pros and Cons of Combining Finances as a Couple
   How to Keep Things Separate
   How to Fairly Allocate Financial Duties and Tasks
   Monthly Budgeting for Couples

Conclusion   135

References   137

Introduction

Have you ever envisioned a life where love and wealth coexist in perfect harmony? Where financial discussions with your partner don't incite battles but instead serve as bridges to understanding? Picture a world where your shared dreams and aspirations drive your financial decisions, bringing you closer rather than pushing you apart.

If you're here, you're part of a community of couples longing to embark on a journey toward building wealth together. This community shares a common experience–one that's echoed in a recent comprehensive survey conducted among couples, revealing an astounding 64% of respondents openly acknowledging what can be termed 'financial incompatibility' within their relationships (Epperson, 2023). This disclosure sheds light on a pervasive challenge many couples face, where distinct financial perspectives, habits, and attitudes become sources of tension and discord in their unions.

Do any of these scenarios resonate with you?

- It's hard to talk about money without fighting.

- You and your partner don't understand each other's ideas about money, and it's tough to plan together.

- Talking about money makes you upset, and you feel blamed or ashamed.

- You're scared about not having enough money, and it's hurting your relationship.

- Figuring out money when your family is unique is confusing, and you can't find the right advice.

Within the following pages, we will delve deep into what it truly means to amass wealth as a couple. We'll explore the emotional triggers and psychological mindsets that often steer our financial choices. We'll equip you with effective communication techniques to discuss finances without casting blame or invoking shame. And most significantly, we will guide you in fashioning a shared financial plan filled with common goals and a roadmap to financial freedom.

As you embark on this journey, you'll gain access to a wealth of shortcuts that will help you and your partner to:

- Quickly find and deal with each other's emotional triggers and thoughts about money, which will help you both understand and care for each other better.

- Learn proven ways to talk about money without fighting, avoiding common mistakes that lead to arguments or hard feelings.

- Easily combine your own money values, goals, and habits into a shared money plan that makes sense for both of you.

- Navigate different money situations and family setups with advice tailored to your specific relationship.

- Speed up your progress toward shared money goals by following a plan made just for couples.

- Build a stronger, happier relationship by working together toward money, success, and freedom.

You'll also be equipped with a comprehensive step-by-step personal finance guide that focuses on these three goals:

1. **Understanding Our Emotional Triggers and Mindset About Money–** In this stage, you'll explore the feelings and thoughts connected to money, becoming skilled at recognizing and addressing both your partner's and your own money-related triggers. This lays the foundation for better money conversations, nurturing mutual understanding and empathy.

2. **Effective Money Communication–** How to Discuss Money Without Conflict or Blame: This section centers on open and collaborative communication. You'll learn methods to discuss finances without arguments and to find common ground. By harmonizing your individual financial values, goals, and behaviors into a unified plan, you ensure both partners are working toward a shared vision.

3. **Creating a Financial Plan Together–** Progressing Toward Financial Freedom: In the final phase, you'll construct a customized financial plan that accounts for your unique situation and relationship dynamics. Follow a roadmap specially crafted for couples as you collaborate to reach your shared financial goals. This process not only strengthens your bond but also fosters harmony in your relationship.

By putting this three-part plan into action, you're on the journey toward building a more robust and financially secure relationship with your partner.

My promise is straightforward: By applying the methods and strategies in this book, you'll experience improved communication, reduced financial stress, and a fortified relationship. Together, you'll work towards your shared economic aspirations, savoring a harmonious and secure financial future.

What do you truly desire? A relationship marked by harmony and ease when it comes to money and financial matters, where your partner fully comprehends your financial perspective? This book holds the key to unlocking those desires.

You seek a guide that is inclusive, empathetic, and tailored to your unique relationship dynamics. You simply want actionable steps to help you surmount the challenges of discussing and managing finances together. Your life goals are unmistakable: building wealth, achieving financial freedom, and nurturing a healthy, joyful relationship.

You often hear the cliché: you can never have enough money. Well, the same goes for love. Do you want to create abundance in your relationship *and* your bank account? If so, financial stability and relationship happiness can coexist like two inseparable lovers.

It's time to embark on this voyage together—a journey towards the romance of wealth and the joy of shaping your future side by side.

Unlocking Your Journey: Get Ready to Transform Your Mindset and Supercharge Your Relationships

Great news! This book prioritizes a smoother reading experience, with longer chapters neatly split into sections. This isn't just an ordinary read; it's your ticket to a transformed mindset and supercharged relationships. Get ready for an incredible journey of personal growth and enriched connections!

Arjun's Story

Once there was a man named Arjun, an astute investor known for his data-driven decisions. However, Arjun's clarity was clouded when he inherited his father's old watch company, a business that had been declining for years. Despite the market research suggesting that investing further in the company would not be fruitful, Arjun's emotions took the helm.

His father had built the company from scratch, and it held a special place in Arjun's heart. He remembered the golden days when his father would come home with stories of new designs and happy customers. To Arjun, this company was not just a business; it was a legacy, a memory of his father's dedication and passion.

Driven by nostalgia, Arjun decided to inject a significant portion of his savings into the company, determined to revive it. He introduced modern designs and invested in aggressive marketing campaigns, hoping to capture the essence of the past while appealing to contemporary tastes.

Months passed, and the emotional gamble did not pay off. The market had shifted too much, and nostalgia was not enough to compete with advanced technology and changing consumer preferences. Arjun's emotional decision led to financial strain, but it also taught him a valuable lesson. He realized that while emotions are an essential part of who we are, they can cloud our judgment in critical matters, especially when it comes to business and investments.

From then on, Arjun vowed to honor his emotions but not let them dictate his financial decisions. He learned to seek balance, remembering his father's resilience in the face of adversity, and applied it to his investment strategies, blending emotional intelligence with financial acumen.

CHAPTER 1

MONEY TALK: EXPLORING YOUR EMOTIONAL RELATIONSHIP WITH WEALTH

Did you know that your beliefs about money, shaped by your upbringing and experiences, directly influence how you manage your finances and interact with your partner about money matters? In this captivating chapter, we delve deep into the intricate web of our personal money mindset. What drives our financial decisions? How do our beliefs about money shape our actions?

As you embark on this enlightening journey, consider this: Can you pinpoint the origins of your own money mindset? Do your early experiences with money still influence your choices today? And, perhaps most crucially, how does your money mindset align with your partner's? Are your financial values in harmony or discord, and how might this impact your shared financial future? It's time to unravel the mysteries of your financial psyche, exploring the power of perception, experience, and emotion in shaping the financial tapestry of your life.

Money Scripts: Understanding the Common Internal Narratives that Drive Financial Behavior and Decision-Making

The concept of "Money Scripts" was introduced by Brad Klontz, a prominent figure in the realm of financial therapy. Essentially, these are the deeply ingrained, unconscious beliefs we hold about money, often rooted in our formative years, and they exert a profound influence on our adult financial behaviors and perspectives (Clarity Wealth Development, 2021).

Consider this common illustration: Individuals who came of age during the Great Depression frequently developed a lifelong inclination towards simplicity and an unwavering concern for saving, even if they later found themselves in a comfortable financial position. It seemed that no matter their financial stability, they grappled with justifying any expenditure.

Now, if we were to pose the question, "What is your earliest memory related to money?" – your response would offer a crucial clue about the origins of your own money script.

The Four Main Types of Money Scripts

There are four main types of money scripts as follows (Clarity Wealth Development, 2021):

Money Avoidance

My dad always told me he believed money is the root of all evil; maybe that's why he never had any. The Bible verse from which this phrase comes actually refers to the love of money being a problem. However, without this subtle distinction, this belief can create an avoidance of money.

Here are some common beliefs among those in this group:

- **Skepticism Toward Wealth:** Some believe that all affluent individuals are inherently driven by greed.

- **Virtue in Poverty:** Another familiar script posits that people with fewer financial means possess a moral purity that is lacking in those with wealth.

- **Emphasis on Giving:** For some, the adage "better to give than receive" is a guiding principle that influences their financial decisions and behaviors.

These deeply ingrained money scripts can significantly shape one's attitudes and actions towards money, offering a window into the complexities of one's financial mindset.

Money Worship

Moving to the opposite end of the spectrum, we encounter the Money Worship category. Individuals in this group view money as a key to stability, seeking it as a means to fill emotional voids or secure their future. However, their approach often involves more than just accumulating wealth; they might mistakenly indulge in overspending, thinking that acquiring more possessions equates to greater happiness. Here are some common money scripts associated with Money Worship:

- Belief in the power of money to control situations.

- Seeing money as a gateway to freedom.

- The idea that acquiring a particular item will finally bring lasting happiness.

Money Status

While individuals in the Money Worship category often use money as a form of emotional relief, those falling into the Money Status category closely tie their self-esteem to their financial worth. They perceive themselves as superior if they possess more material possessions than others. Here are some typical money scripts associated with the Money Status category:

- A belief that not acquiring the latest technology equates to falling behind in life.

- The conviction that wealth leads to greater happiness.

Money Vigilance

Among the four categories, the Money Vigilance group represents a relatively balanced approach, although it can sometimes become overly strict. These individuals regularly assess their spending and saving habits, aiming to make prudent financial choices. It seems sensible, doesn't it? However, some take it to an extreme, denying themselves the enjoyment of what their money could provide due to their unwavering vigilance in overspending. Here are a couple of common money scripts associated with Money Vigilance:

- A strict aversion to using credit for purchases.
- The belief that the satisfaction of saving money surpasses the pleasure of buying things.

The Role of Upbringing and Culture in Shaping Our Money Mindset

We typically recognize that our family, socio-economic background, and culture contribute to the development of our beliefs, but did you realize that this is also true for our economic beliefs and our inherent money mindset?

Financial Times speaks of Alice, a 28-year-old healthcare manager from London, who had a unique way of handling her money. Even though she earned £80,000 a year and was well-educated, her financial behavior puzzled researchers. She freely spent money on nights out using her credit card but regularly sent money to her parents for safekeeping. Surprisingly, she considered her pension a backup plan but didn't trust it.

Instead, she believed her home was a secure source of wealth, even though house prices had been unstable in recent years. To Alice, her mortgage was considered productive debt, while her credit card debt was viewed as indulgent. This might seem odd from a traditional financial perspective, which often relies on concepts like portfolio risk and rational expectations, assuming money operates consistently like the laws of physics (Tett, 2021). One would wonder how many people think like Alice and why. This is where a deeper look into one's upbringing and culture comes in.

Key Factors Shaping Your Money Mindset

In line with the impact of culture and background on how people view and treat money, let's zero in on some of the major factors that shape people's money mindsets (Finvision Financial Services, 2023):

Childhood Experiences: The way you were exposed to money and finances during childhood can significantly impact your money mindset. For instance, if you were raised in a family with limited financial resources, you might have developed the perception that money is nearly impossible to attain.

Cultural and Social Influences: Your money mindset can also be influenced by cultural and social elements, including media, family, friends, and societal norms. For example, if you grew up in a culture that prioritizes thriftiness and saving, you might have adopted the belief that spending money is extravagant.

Education and Learning: Education and acquiring knowledge can play a role in shaping your money mindset. For instance, if you've been educated about the benefits of investing and compound interest, you might have developed the belief that you can build wealth gradually.

Personal Experiences: Your personal financial achievements and setbacks can directly influence your money mindset. For instance, you may be skeptical of taking financial risks if you've gone through some setbacks or losses in that area.

By comprehending the factors that contribute to your money mindset, you can work towards cultivating a more constructive and optimistic perspective on money.

The Influence of Your Mindset on Your Finances and Your Relationship

Your money mindset shapes how you handle money and feel about it. Even more vital to understand is that a positive mindset leads to better financial choices and success. When you reflect on your beliefs about money, do you find that you take money seriously or think it's only for the born-wealthy? Changing your mindset can improve your financial success, and no one else can do it for you. Start by understanding the idea of a money mindset to cultivate a healthier and positive approach to money.

Money Mindset Defined

A money mindset is how someone thinks and acts when it comes to money. It includes their beliefs, attitudes, and behaviors about wealth. A good money mindset means having positive thoughts about money and seeing it as a way to reach your goals and have a happy life. This mindset affects how you make money choices, manage your finances, and meet your money needs. People with a healthy money mindset are mindful of their spending and work towards their financial goals.

Evaluating and Sharing Money Mindsets in Couples

Understanding and aligning your money mindsets as a couple is essential for building a healthy financial future together. Here is an overview of the steps needed to help you assess each other's money mindset and bridge any gaps in perspective:

- **Open Communication:** Start by fostering an environment of open and honest communication. Create a safe space where both partners can freely express their thoughts and feelings about money without judgment. Encourage each other to share personal experiences and beliefs related to finances.

- **Self-Reflection:** Each partner should take time for self-reflection. Identify your own money scripts, beliefs, and attitudes about money. Consider how your upbringing, past experiences, and cultural influences have shaped your financial perspective.

- **Active Listening:** Actively listen to your partner's financial stories and viewpoints. Pay attention to their emotions and triggers related to money. Avoid interrupting or passing judgment during this process. Seek to understand rather than to persuade.

- **Discuss Differences:** It's natural for couples to have differences in their money mindsets. Embrace these distinctions as opportunities for growth rather than sources of conflict. Discuss where your perspectives may differ and why.

- **Set Mutual Goals:** Find common ground by setting mutual financial goals. This could include short-term objectives like saving for a vacation or long-term goals like buying a home or planning for retirement. Aligning on shared financial aspirations can help bridge mindset gaps.

- **Financial Education:** Invest in financial education together. Attend workshops, read books, or consult a financial advisor as a team. This not only enhances your financial literacy but also encourages collaboration in managing your finances.

- **Regular Check-Ins:** Money mindsets can evolve over time. Schedule regular check-ins to revisit your financial discussions and reassess your shared goals. Be open to adjusting your financial strategies as needed.

We'll keep coming back to these key points throughout the book and go into greater detail about how to apply them in your life. By following these steps, you and your partner can gain a deeper understanding of each other's money mindset, foster empathy, and work together toward financial harmony and shared prosperity.

Activity: Money Mindset Quiz for Couples

Instructions: This quiz is designed to help you and your partner better understand your individual money mindsets. Money can be a sensitive topic, but it's essential to have open and honest discussions about your financial beliefs and values. Answer the following questions independently and then compare your answers to spark meaningful conversations about your financial goals and priorities.

Scoring: Choose the option that best represents your viewpoint for each question. Assign points based on your choices, with 1 point for option A, 2 points for option B, and 3 points for option C. Add up your scores at the end to determine your money mindset type.

Questions:

When it comes to budgeting and spending money:
A. I prefer to save as much as possible, even if it means cutting back on fun activities.
B. I like to balance saving and spending, making sure we enjoy life while planning for the future.
C. I believe in spending money to create memorable experiences, and I don't stress too much about saving.

When unexpected expenses arise, how do you typically react?
A. I get anxious and worry about how it will affect our financial stability.
B. I assess the situation, adjust our budget if necessary, and find ways to cover

the expense.
C. I view it as a temporary setback and try to find a solution without stressing too much.

How comfortable are you with sharing financial details and discussing money openly with your partner?
A. I'm uncomfortable sharing too many financial details and prefer to handle money matters on my own.
B. I'm open to discussing finances but might avoid certain topics to prevent arguments.
C. I believe in complete financial transparency and think it's crucial for a healthy relationship.

What do you think about taking on debt (e.g., loans, credit cards) to achieve financial goals?
A. I'm strongly against taking on debt and believe in paying cash for everything.
B. I think some types of debt can be useful if managed responsibly to achieve important goals.
C. I don't mind taking on debt if it helps us reach our goals faster, but I'm careful not to overspend.

How do you approach financial planning for the long-term (e.g., retirement, investments)?
A. I'm very conservative and prioritize saving for retirement above all else.
B. I balance saving for the long term with enjoying life in the present.
C. I'm more focused on enjoying life now and believe the future will work itself out.

When you and your partner have a disagreement about money, how do you handle it?
A. I tend to avoid conflict and may give in to keep the peace.
B. We discuss our differing opinions and try to find a compromise.
C. I stand my ground and believe my perspective is the right one.

How do you define financial success in your relationship?
A. Having a large savings account and being debt-free.
B. Achieving a balance between financial security and enjoying life together.
C. Creating memorable experiences and not worrying too much about money.

Now, calculate your scores:
Total points for Option A: _____
Total points for Option B: _____
Total points for Option C: _____

Results:

- **7-12 points:** The Conservative Saver. You tend to prioritize financial stability and saving over spending. Open communication with your partner is essential to find a balance that works for both of you.

- **13-18 points:** The Balanced Planner. You strike a healthy balance between saving for the future and enjoying the present. Continue to work together to ensure your financial goals align.

- **19-21 points:** The Free Spirit. You believe in living in the moment and value experiences over strict financial planning. Make sure you and your partner are on the same page regarding your financial aspirations.

Chapter 1 has taken us on a fascinating journey into the depths of our financial psyche. Who knew that our childhood memories about money and societal influences could have such a profound impact on our financial decisions? As we bid adieu to this chapter, let's take a moment to reflect on the key takeaways:

- **Money Scripts and Their Influence:** Money Scripts are those hidden beliefs about money, often shaped during our formative years, that continue to guide our financial choices. Understanding your Money Script is the first step to gaining control over your financial life.

- **Your Background Matters:** Your upbringing, culture, and personal experiences all play a significant role in shaping your money mindset. The way you were exposed to money during childhood can have a lasting impact on your relationship with finances.

- **Money Mindset and Its Impact:** Your money mindset shapes your financial behavior, and a positive mindset can lead to better financial decisions and success. Whether you take money seriously or view it as an exclusive club for the ultra-wealthy is a mindset that can be changed.

- **Evaluating and Sharing Money Mindsets as a Couple:** Open and honest communication about your financial beliefs is key. Embrace differences as opportunities for growth rather than sources of conflict. Setting mutual financial goals and investing in financial education as a team can bridge mindset gaps.

Now that you're armed with a deeper understanding of your money mindset, take a moment to reflect on your own beliefs about money and how they align with your partner's. Engage in meaningful conversations and remain open to adjusting your financial strategies as needed.

Remember, your financial journey as a couple is a dynamic one, and it's perfectly normal for money mindsets to evolve over time. Keep the lines of communication open and be prepared to adapt to new financial goals and aspirations as they arise. As we move forward in this book, we'll explore strategies and practices to help you and your partner realize your shared financial dreams and navigate the intricacies of managing money as a team. Stay tuned and keep the financial conversations flowing!

Ella's Story

In the heart of a bustling city lived a woman named Ella, who found solace in the gleaming windows of the shopping district whenever clouds of gloom loomed over her. On one such day, burdened with the weight of a hard week, Ella drifted into her favorite boutique, the colors and textures promising a taste of happiness.

Each shop wooed her with colors and styles that lit up her imagination. With every silk scarf and every glittering accessory she touched, a slice of her sadness was replaced by a rush of momentary joy. The soft hum of the store's music seemed to harmonize with her rising spirits, and before she knew it, Ella was at the counter, her arms laden with bags, her heart momentarily light.

It was only when she returned home, the high of retail therapy fading, that Ella faced the sea of glossy bags and felt a pang of regret. The beautiful things she'd brought home couldn't fill the void of loneliness she was trying to escape. Ella realized then that while shopping had given her a quick escape, it was the warmth of genuine happiness she truly yearned for, something that couldn't be bought or owned.

From that day on, Ella sought healthier ways to cope with her lows. She still visited the boutiques, but instead of shopping to soothe her soul, she did it to celebrate life's highs, finding that true contentment came from within, not from a shopping spree.

Chapter 2

The Financial Heartstrings: How Money Affects Your Emotions

"I don't have a therapist; I have the mall," my friend Shelia told me over coffee. She was joking about using shopping as a coping mechanism for dealing with life's stresses and struggles, but I knew how her impulsive spending had caused many fights between her and her partner. While laying out that credit card for a shiny new toy feels soothing in the moment, the dread of her partner's judgment and the guilt of adding another unnecessary possession to her brimming closet quickly drowns out the temporary relief of shopping therapy.

We all make impulse purchases from time to time, but we often overlook the significant impact of our emotions on our financial decisions.

Let's uncover the hidden connections between fear, guilt, shame, and money in this revealing chapter.

The Interplay of Fear, Guilt, and Shame: Unraveling Their Impact on Financial Decision-Making

We all share a complex relationship with money at some point in our lives. While we understand the importance of creating and adhering to a financial plan, we often find ourselves succumbing to impulsive spending. Whether it's the guilt that follows overspending or the fear and guilt that lead us to deny ourselves basic necessities, one thing is certain–our financial decisions are undeniably intertwined with a range of negative emotions.

When you make decisions about money, they have a direct impact on your financial situation or even status. Consequently, these impacts influence your feelings or emotions and, in turn, your future behaviors. Can you see how much of a vicious cycle this can easily become?

When it comes to the psychology behind our personal relationship with money, there are often three constant factors involved (Gourguechon, 2019):

- Emotions wield significant influence whether we realize it or not.
- Anxiety and avoidance perpetuate a harmful cycle.
- Psychologically, your family and past are inescapable to some extent.

Emotions and Money

Let's get into a more detailed explanation of how our negative feelings and emotions affect our financial goals (Hakeenah, 2021):

Guilt

In financial matters, guilt is a prominent emotion that can manifest in various ways. People tend to experience guilt when they have too much compared to their peers, neglect personal finances, or keep money-related secrets.

Moreover, when one engages in activities that delay or hinder their financial goals, they may experience an overwhelming sense of guilt. These activities manifest in various forms, including impulsive spending, off-budget donations, or delaying crucial decisions.

However, while guilt is a negative emotion, it can also prompt positive changes like revising budgets and practicing better money management.

What to do

Begin by forgiving yourself for past mistakes and accepting that you can't change the past. If necessary, confess and clear your conscience to move forward in your financial journey. Remember that keeping financial secrets may hinder intimacy with your partner, and it's not worth it in the long run.

Identify the sources and triggers of your guilt, such as earning more money than your partner, making poor financial decisions in the past, or accumulating debt. Begin to establish a healthier relationship with money by empowering yourself through financial education (as you are doing right now!), developing clear and open communication with your partner, and proactively starting to replace negative money habits with positive ones. We'll talk more in the pages ahead about setting specific goals for habit change and establishing realistic timelines for achieving them.

Fear

Common financial fears include concerns about insufficient funds, the fear of being misjudged for displaying wealth, the apprehension of making financial mistakes, and the dread of exposure or humiliation. This is a toxic emotion, and addressing its root cause is crucial before it clouds your judgment. It affects your financial health, and it often materializes as the fear of losing all your assets, facing bankruptcy, perpetual economic scarcity, or even fear of success.

What to do

Sooner or later, fear will paralyze your decision-making process, making it vital to recognize and address the anxieties surrounding money. A dedicated journal for your financial concerns can help identify and track your money-related fears, paving the way for effective strategies to eliminate them, which may also involve seeking professional guidance.

Being intentional about shifting your money-related thought patterns is crucial. Begin by recognizing your risk tolerance and align your investments accordingly. If you have a low-risk tolerance, prioritize less risky ventures. As you gain confidence over time, you can incrementally transition from low-risk investments and feel more comfortable exploring opportunities that previously felt too daunting.

Shame

In our family, money disputes were rooted in the deepest corners of shame. Each financial argument was a battle to conceal our financial struggles, an unspoken agreement to keep up appearances. The shame we carried silently spoke louder than any words exchanged, fueling tensions, and pushing us further apart. It was a story we all knew but were afraid to confront.

While guilt revolves around the adverse impact of financial decisions on others, shame primarily concerns failing to meet one's own financial goals. It's an influential emotion in personal finance, capable of derailing necessary money-related actions.

Shame often triggers the instinct to hide what one is ashamed of, a feeling I was too familiar with growing up. It often leads to behaviors like avoiding thoughts of finances, neglecting budgeting and savings, and using spending as a form of therapy. Recognizing shame in your money management is crucial, as unaddressed shame can divert your focus from your financial objectives. This becomes especially problematic when you lack defined financial goals, leaving you without a starting point or destination.

What to do

To free yourself from shame, pinpoint the sources of your money-related shame and confront them head-on. Cultivate a habit of meticulous financial planning to eliminate the triggers of financial shame.

Moreover, forgive yourself, as acknowledging the impact of shame on your finances signifies progress in addressing past money errors. Embrace the lessons from those mistakes as stepping stones toward a brighter financial future.

The Influence of Financial Upbringing on Current Money Management Habits

As we've discussed, our relationship with money is deeply rooted in our upbringing and early experiences. For me, understanding the influence of my financial upbringing on my current money management habits has been a journey of self-awareness and transformation.

Growing up, money was a constant source of tension in my family. I vividly remember the heated arguments about bills, debt, and the struggle to make ends meet. These experiences left an indelible mark on my psyche, shaping my initial approach to money.

In my early adult years, I found myself mirroring the financial anxieties and disputes I had witnessed in my family. I struggled to manage my finances, often feeling overwhelmed by bills and financial responsibilities. It was a cycle that I desperately wanted to break.

Self-awareness became the catalyst for change. I realized that my upbringing had instilled certain beliefs and behaviors around money. I understood that I had the power to alter my money management habits and forge a healthier relationship with finances.

I began by seeking knowledge and education on personal finance. I devoured books, attended workshops, and sought advice from financial experts. Over time, I cultivated practical skills in budgeting, saving, and investing. These steps, combined with my newfound self-awareness, allowed me to make more informed financial decisions.

Today, I can proudly say that my financial upbringing no longer dictates my money management habits. Instead, I've taken control of my financial well-being. I've transformed from a person who saw money as a source of stress into someone who views it as a tool for building a secure and fulfilling future.

This journey has taught me the profound impact of self-awareness and education in reshaping our relationship with money. It's a testament to the fact that our past need not define our financial future. By recognizing the influence of our upbringing and actively working to change our money mindset, we can take charge of our financial destinies and build a more prosperous and harmonious life.

As we explore the potential influence of your background on your money management skills, please consider my own journey as a reminder that change is possible. Recognizing the impact of your financial upbringing is the first step towards fostering a healthier relationship with money. This transformation isn't just for your benefit alone; it also has the potential to positively impact your partner, children, or others in your immediate circle.

Ways Your Financial Upbringing May Be Manifesting in Your Money-Management Skills

Here are some ways in which the financial environment in which you were raised may influence your current money management habits:

Financial Values and Attitudes: The values your parents or caregivers instilled in you regarding saving, spending, and debt can strongly influence your financial decisions as an adult. If you grew up in a family where frugality and saving were prioritized, you might be more inclined to be a cautious saver. Conversely, if you witnessed a casual approach to spending, you might find it challenging to manage impulse buying.

Budgeting and Financial Literacy: The lessons or lack thereof in budgeting and financial literacy during your upbringing can directly impact your ability to manage money effectively. If financial discussions were open and educational in your family, you may have a better grasp of budgeting. Conversely, if money matters were rarely discussed or kept behind secretive closed doors, you might find yourself struggling with basic financial concepts.

Debt Management: Observing how your family handled debt, such as credit cards or loans, can influence your own approach to debt management. If your family was cautious about accumulating debt, you might be more debt averse. On the other hand, if debt was managed casually, you might be more prone to haphazardly accumulating debt without a clear repayment strategy.

Financial Anxiety and Conflict: If your family experienced financial stress and conflict, this could have lasting effects on your own financial anxiety and conflict resolution skills. Witnessing frequent arguments about money might make you more prone to financial stress and money-talk avoidance and less equipped to handle financial disagreements with your partner.

Investment and Wealth Building: The exposure to or absence of investment discussions and wealth-building strategies in your family can significantly influence your approach to growing wealth. If your family emphasized investment and wealth-building strategies, you might be more likely to engage in these activities. Otherwise, you could lack the expertise or self-assurance required to initiate the investment process.

Understanding the impact of your financial upbringing is the first step in recognizing how it might be influencing your current money management habits. This awareness empowers you to make intentional changes, develop healthier financial habits, and create a more secure financial future for yourself and those around you.

Navigating Financial Differences: Common Conflicts in Couples with Differing Values, Goals, and Priorities

When two individuals come together in a relationship, they bring their unique perspectives, beliefs, and experiences, including those related to money. These differences in financial values, goals, and priorities can be a significant source of both tension and growth in a partnership.

It's time to delve into the challenges that couples may encounter when their financial perspectives don't perfectly align. Understanding these common conflicts is the first step toward finding solutions and building a stronger, more harmonious financial partnership.

Divergent Spending Habits: Differences in spending styles, such as one partner being a saver and the other a spender, can lead to disagreements about budgeting and financial choices.

Financial Goals Misalignment: When partners have conflicting financial objectives, like one aspiring to save for a home while the other wishes to travel extensively, it can create challenges in reaching a consensus.

Unequal Financial Contributions: Discrepancies in income or contribution to shared expenses may lead to feelings of inequity or resentment and affect the balance in the relationship.

Debt Management Disagreements: Disagreements about handling and paying off debts, such as credit card balances or student loans, can result in financial stress and friction.

Conflict Over Budgeting and Saving: Variances in attitudes toward budgeting and saving can result in disputes over allocating funds for daily expenses and future financial security.

Financial Secrets and Trust Issues: Concealing financial matters or making major financial decisions without the knowledge or consent of one's partner can undermine trust and lead to conflict.

Family Financial Obligations: Disagreements about supporting extended family members financially can lead to intense friction, particularly when it affects the couple's own financial goals.

Investment Disagreements: Conflicting opinions on how to invest or manage assets can create tension, especially when it impacts long-term financial plans.

Inheritance and Legacy Concerns: Disagreements about the use of inheritance or plans for leaving a financial legacy can be emotionally charged and lead to conflict.

Approaches to Emergency Funds: Differences in how to manage and access emergency funds can cause stress when unexpected expenses arise.

Navigating these common conflicts requires open communication, compromise, and a shared commitment to understanding and respecting each other's financial values and priorities.

Harmonizing Financial Values: Tips for Addressing Conflicting Beliefs in Relationships

Many couples have different or conflicting financial values, but that doesn't necessarily mean they're not right for each other. Should conflicting financial beliefs be left to escalate until there's no ounce of peace in the relationship? I don't believe so. In fact, addressing these differences head-on and finding common ground can not only resolve conflicts but also strengthen the bond between partners. On that basis, we must explore strategies and insights to help you and your partner navigate the complex terrain of financial disparities.

By recognizing the importance of communication, compromise, and mutual respect, you can turn financial conflicts into opportunities for growth, understanding, and a more harmonious partnership. Let's take a look at these simple and yet powerful strategies (Brown, 2021):

Have Open Conversations About Finances with Your Partner

Money itself is rarely the root cause of relationship discord; instead, poor communication about financial matters is what leads to strife. This communication breakdown can escalate to a relationship breakdown, including divorce. However, open discussions about money can foster a deeper understanding, acceptance, and respect for your partner.

Kathleen Burns Kingsbury, a Wealth Psychology Expert and host of the Breaking Money Silence® podcast, emphasizes that money often mirrors the dynamics within a relationship, serving as a means to express unconscious emotions, be it love, control, anger, or more (Brown, 2021). Partners who collaborate on financial decisions, work through money conflicts, and share common goals are more likely to operate as a team, respecting differences and shared values. Conversely, secrecy around money can signify conflict avoidance or secrecy in other areas of the relationship.

To start this open dialogue, establish your financial goals and approach your partner with an open mind. Instead of trying to persuade your significant other to adopt your perspective, recognize that each of your viewpoints may differ, offering a learning opportunity.

Hugh Massie, a pioneer in Behavioral Finance Insights, suggests that both partners should first understand their individual identities and goals. Once they've done that, they can work towards creating an interdependent life rather than a codependent one, making healthier financial decisions and preventing money from becoming a barrier (Brown, 2021).

Consider seeking money counseling for couples, as a third party can often facilitate resolving financial issues in a marriage. Their impartial perspective can be instrumental in addressing challenging financial situations.

Evaluate Your Financial Values and Boundaries

In the pursuit of harmonizing financial values and mitigating conflicting beliefs within a relationship, evaluating your own ideals and setting clear boundaries emerge as pivotal strategies. First, take the time to assess your individual financial values and encourage your partner to do the same. This self-awareness lays the groundwork for understanding potential areas of divergence. The next step is engaging in candid, judgment-free conversations with your partner about your financial values. Listen attentively to their perspective, fostering an environment of respect and open communication.

Moreover, identifying common ground between your financial values is essential. Uncover shared goals or priorities, using these as a solid foundation for your financial decisions. Let's consider an example: Tre and Alex, a couple who initially had opposing views on spending and saving and generally avoided the topic of money altogether. After realizing this avoidance was causing distance between them, they sat down together to get their concerns about finances out on the table. Through this open discussion, they realized that each of them valued financial security but had different approaches to achieving it. By finding common ground in their shared goal of financial stability, they were able to align their strategies and strengthen their partnership. While differences may exist, focusing on the areas of agreement can create unity in your financial journey.

Setting distinct financial boundaries is also key; determine which financial decisions are acceptable or not in your relationship, such as requiring joint approval for significant purchases. Regularly revisit and adjust these boundaries as your financial values evolve, ensuring you remain aligned and can address potential conflicts proactively. This approach fosters a deeper understanding and mutual respect, paving the way for a harmonious and financially secure partnership.

Address Power Imbalances

Nothing exposes power imbalances in relationships like money does. Financial disparities can often amplify existing imbalances, leading to tension and conflict. To foster a healthy and equitable financial partnership, it's crucial to address and rectify these power differentials.

The first step in addressing power imbalances is recognizing and acknowledging their existence. This might entail examining the division of financial responsibilities, decision-making authority, or control over resources within your relationship.

Engage in open and honest communication with your partner about how financial power is distributed. Encourage them to share their feelings and concerns regarding these imbalances. A supportive and non-judgmental environment is essential for this conversation.

Collaborate with your partner to identify and implement equitable solutions, such as redistributing financial responsibilities or jointly making significant financial decisions. Strive to ensure that both partners have an equal say in financial matters.

Define shared financial goals that both partners are invested in, shifting the focus from individual power dynamics to collaborative financial planning. Having mutual objectives fosters a sense of unity. In some cases, seeking the guidance of a financial counselor or therapist can be beneficial. A neutral third party can help you navigate complex power imbalances and work towards fair resolutions.

Power dynamics can change over time, so it's essential to conduct regular check-ins to ensure that power imbalances do not reemerge. Revisiting your financial arrangements and decision-making processes periodically is a proactive way to maintain equity.

Navigating Income Shortfalls Together

Income shortfalls can be a challenging and stressful experience for couples, as they can put financial stability and the strength of a relationship to the test. However, by approaching these situations as a team and with open communication, couples can successfully navigate income shortfalls while strengthening their bond. Here are some key strategies to help you and your partner through these financial storms together:

Open and Honest Communication: Yes, I can't emphasize this point enough, which is why it keeps recurring. The cornerstone of managing income shortfalls is open and honest communication. Share your concerns, fears, and financial realities with your partner. Discuss your priorities and long-term goals. This sets the stage for understanding and empathy.

Assess Your Financial Situation: Take a close look at your financial situation. Determine the extent of the income shortfall and how long it might last. Understanding the full scope of the problem allows you to make informed decisions.

Create a Budget: Together, create a revised budget that reflects your current income. Identify essential expenses, prioritize them, and cut non-essential spending. A budget ensures you're both on the same page regarding financial decisions.

Emergency Fund and Savings: If you have an emergency fund or savings, now may be the time to use it. It's what it's there for. Discuss the best way to access and use these funds while maintaining a safety net.

Seek Additional Income: Explore opportunities to increase your income, such as part-time work, freelancing, or selling unused items. Doing this together can foster a sense of unity and teamwork.

Credit and Debt Management: If necessary, discuss the responsible use of credit or loans to cover essential expenses during the shortfall. Understand the implications of taking on debt and create a repayment plan.

Prioritize Essential Expenses: Ensure that you have a shared understanding of what constitutes essential expenses. This may include housing, utilities, groceries, and healthcare. Agree on where to cut back.

Support Each Other Emotionally: Income shortfalls can lead to stress and anxiety. Be supportive and understanding of each other's emotional reactions. Create a safe space to express your concerns without judgment.

Explore Government Assistance: Depending on the nature of the income shortfall, investigate whether you qualify for government assistance or relief programs. This can be a temporary lifeline during difficult times.

Long-Term Financial Planning: Use the experience of navigating an income shortfall as a catalyst for long-term financial planning. Discuss building a stronger financial foundation, increasing savings, and ensuring financial security for the future.

Regular Check-Ins: Continuously reassess your financial situation as it evolves. Regular check-ins allow you to make adjustments as necessary and stay aligned with your financial goals.

Celebrate Small Wins: Acknowledge and celebrate each milestone you achieve while dealing with the income shortfall. Whether it's successfully sticking to your budget or finding additional income, recognizing your progress can be motivating.

In times of financial hardship, couples who work together, communicate openly, and support each other emotionally tend to emerge stronger. Navigating income shortfalls can be a challenging journey, but it can also be an opportunity to deepen your connection and demonstrate your commitment to each other's well-being.

Chapter 2 delved into the intricate relationship between emotions and financial decisions. It uncovered the hidden connections between fear, guilt, shame, and money, highlighting how these emotions can significantly affect our financial choices. In this chapter, you explored the interplay of these emotions and their impact on your financial decision-making. Let's recap the crucial points:

- **Emotional Influence:** Emotions play a pivotal role in financial decisions, creating a cycle of reactions that can have lasting effects on your financial situation and status.

- **Managing Guilt:** Guilt often arises from activities that hinder financial goals, like impulsive spending or delaying crucial decisions. However, guilt can also catalyze positive changes, such as revising budgets and practicing better money management.

- **Overcoming Fear:** Fear can manifest in various ways, including concerns about insufficient funds or the fear of making financial mistakes. Addressing the root causes of fear and shifting your money-related thought patterns are key to managing this emotion effectively.

- **Confronting Shame:** Shame primarily concerns the failure to meet your own financial goals and can lead to behaviors like neglecting budgeting and savings. Recognizing and addressing the sources of shame and embracing the lessons from past mistakes are essential steps in overcoming this emotion.

- **Financial Upbringing:** We explored the influence of your financial upbringing on your current money management habits and learned that your early experiences with money can leave a lasting mark on your financial behavior. Self-awareness and education are powerful tools for transformation.

- **Couples and Financial Differences:** This chapter also highlighted the common conflicts couples may face when their financial perspectives don't align perfectly. Divergent spending habits, financial goals misalignment, and other issues can challenge a partnership.

- **Strategies for Harmonizing Financial Values:** To address these differences, the chapter provided strategies for fostering open communication, evaluating financial values and boundaries, and tackling power imbalances in a relationship.

- **Navigating Income Shortfalls Together:** This chapter offered key strategies for dealing with income shortfalls as a team, emphasizing the importance of open and honest communication, budgeting, and prioritizing essential expenses.

I hope this chapter helped you better understand the emotional aspects of financial decision-making and discover strategies to foster financial harmony in your relationship. Your financial journey as a couple is dynamic, so staying open to evolving money mindsets and adapting to new financial goals is essential as you continue through the book.

Nora and Ben's Story

Nora and Ben seemed to be a couple that neighbors envied—two peas in a pod with laughter often spilling from the windows of their cozy townhouse. But beneath the surface, there brewed a storm of mistrust that threatened to uproot their relationship's very foundation.

Ben, a freelance graphic designer, had always been somewhat elusive about his earnings, but Nora, a schoolteacher, trusted him implicitly. They had their shared accounts and individual accounts for personal expenses, a system that had worked for years—or so Nora thought.

It was during a routine check of their joint savings for a planned vacation that Nora stumbled upon transactions she couldn't account for. Expensive electronics, nights at high-end restaurants, and even a membership to a luxury gym—none of which she had ever seen or heard about from Ben.

The confrontation was quiet but intense, taking place over the dinner table where they had shared plans and dreams. Nora's hands trembled, not just from anger but from a sense of betrayal as she held up the bank statements. "Why, Ben?" was all she could muster.

Ben's face was a canvas of regret. He had been selfish, indulging in pleasures while spinning a web of lies, thinking it harmless if Nora never found out. But as the truth hung heavy between them, he realized the cost was not just monetary. He had gambled with something far more valuable—their trust.

It took time for the couple to navigate this storm. Financial infidelity, as they learned to call it, had rocked their boat, but they were determined not to let it sink. They sought the help of a financial advisor and a counselor to rebuild their financial health and trust, respectively. Every step forward was a brick in the wall of trust they were reconstructing.

NORA AND BEN'S STORY

Through open conversations, full disclosure of finances, and setting new, transparent ground rules, they slowly mended the fissures. Their journey was not without setbacks, but with each shared monthly budget review and each honest dialogue, they were not just repairing, but also fortifying their relationship.

CHAPTER 3

FINANCIALLY IN SYNC: HOW TO ALIGN YOUR MONEY VALUES AND GOALS TOGETHER

In this chapter, we'll dive into the nitty-gritty of financial alignment within your relationship. No, it's not always as smooth as a love song, but it's a crucial part of achieving financial freedom together. We'll explore the practical steps to sync up your financial values and goals, learn to talk about money openly, and address those pesky fears and hurdles that might be holding you back.

Imagine navigating your financial journey as a team, working together seamlessly. Aligning your economic values and goals is the key to making this a reality. In this chapter, we'll show you how to build a shared financial plan and tackle the obstacles in your way. We'll provide practical steps and strategies you can use to ensure that you and your partner are on the same financial page, working together towards your common goals.

Breaking Down Personal Barriers to Financial Partnership

Now that you've examined your experiences with money as a child or young adult, you may have an idea of your own personal barriers regarding money. Remember that your partner has a different set of financial memories. It's crucial not to offload your financial baggage onto them, as it can lead to misunderstandings, disagreements, and, ultimately, a strained partnership.

For instance, if you grew up in a household where money was always a source of stress and arguments, you might approach every financial discussion with anxiety, anticipating conflict. In contrast, your partner may have had a more carefree upbringing regarding money, and they find your concerns or hesitations perplexing. These differences can create tension within your relationship.

On the flip side, maybe you were raised with the belief that it's important to save every penny, and you feel guilty when you indulge in any non-essential expenses. Your partner, however, might see spending as a means to enjoy life, and they may question your resistance to occasionally splurge on something you both enjoy.

In this chapter, we will explore these personal barriers that stem from your upbringing, past experiences, and unique money beliefs. But we won't leave you hanging with just the challenges; we'll also provide solutions and strategies to help you bridge the gap between your money mindsets.

By identifying and addressing these personal barriers, you can foster a more harmonious financial partnership. You'll learn how to understand each other's money beliefs, communicate effectively, and make financial decisions that align with your shared goals. Before we delve into the strategies for addressing these barriers, it's essential to understand the concept through a few examples (Lorz, 2023). Here are some limiting beliefs about money:

- "I lack the intelligence to make wise investment decisions."

- "My income will never be sufficient to allow for savings."

- "I'll forever remain trapped in the cycle of living paycheck to paycheck."

- "I struggle with managing money effectively."

- "There's never enough money to cover all of my needs and wants."

- "Earning money requires relentless hard work."
- "Money cannot bring happiness or fulfillment."
- "I should only spend money on my family and neglect my own needs and desires."
- "I don't deserve to have more money than I currently do."
- "My worth is determined solely by the amount of money I possess."
- "As soon as I acquire money, it quickly disappears."
- "Only morally questionable individuals desire more wealth."
- "People are only interested in me for my financial resources."
- "My debt makes others view me as unintelligent."

These beliefs can significantly impact one's financial decisions and overall well-being. Addressing and transforming them is a crucial step toward achieving a healthier financial mindset. Here's how you can go about it (Lorz, 2023):

Step 1: Identify Your Money Obstacle for What It Is

Before you can tackle your money block issues, you need to recognize them for what they truly are. This initial step is foundational to the entire process of overcoming limiting beliefs and behaviors related to money.

Why is Identifying Your Money Obstacle Important?

Awareness: Many money obstacles operate subconsciously. You might not even be fully aware that they exist or how they influence your financial decisions. By shining a light on them, you bring them into your conscious awareness.

Clarity: Identifying your money obstacle provides clarity. It's like turning on a light in a dark room, allowing you to see the obstacle clearly. This clarity helps you understand how it has been affecting your financial choices.

Ownership: Recognizing the money block empowers you to take ownership of it. You can acknowledge that it's a part of your financial landscape and that it's been holding you back. This ownership is a crucial step toward change.

Using Silly Interrupters to Snap Out of It

Acknowledging your money obstacle might sound straightforward, but it can be challenging in practice. Our beliefs and behaviors often become deeply ingrained, making them hard to identify and address. This is where "silly interrupters" come in handy.

Silly interrupters are playful tactics you can employ to disrupt your habitual thought patterns. They're like a gentle nudge to remind you to question your beliefs. For instance, if you catch yourself thinking, "I'm terrible with money," you might use a silly interrupter by imagining a comical thought, like, "Am I actually as bad with money as a penguin trying to balance on one foot?" This whimsical humor can help break the cycle of negative self-talk and open the door to self-reflection.

Questioning the Belief

Once you've introduced a silly interrupter, it's time to question the validity of your money block. Ask yourself, "Is this negative belief always 100% true?" The answer should typically be "no." Why? Because very few things in life are universally and unconditionally true. Beliefs about money are often influenced by our experiences, emotions, and external factors, making them subjective and open to interpretation.

Understanding that your money obstacle is not an absolute truth but a conditioned response allows you to reevaluate its impact on your financial decisions.

By identifying your money obstacle, using playful interrupters, and questioning the belief's universality, you pave the way for deeper introspection and transformation. This process will help you address and, ultimately, overcome the money block issues holding you back from achieving your financial goals and true financial freedom.

Step 2: Discover Contradictory Proof

In this pivotal step, we focus on finding evidence that directly challenges your limiting beliefs about money. The purpose is to prove to yourself that there are alternative perspectives and possibilities, allowing you to break free from the shackles of negative financial beliefs.

Why It Matters:

- Your money beliefs might have deep roots, and your life experiences have likely reaffirmed them.

- Actively seeking out contradictory evidence empowers you to see the flip side of your limiting beliefs.

The Process:

- Conduct research and engage in self-reflection.

- Surround yourself with positive influences and seek advice from individuals with healthier money perspectives.

- Practice visualization to create a positive mental image of your financial future.

- Keep a "Contradictory Proof Journal" to record instances that challenge your limiting beliefs.

- Consider professional guidance, such as a financial therapist, for deeply ingrained money blocks.

The Power of Contradictory Proof: Accumulating contradictory evidence will boost your confidence in your ability to change your financial situation. Over time, it reshapes your beliefs, enhances your financial self-efficacy, and propels you toward financial freedom. This step is crucial to your journey toward a healthier financial mindset and more positive money habits.

Step 3: Forgive Yourself

In this essential step, we address the emotional aspect of money block issues, where self-forgiveness is pivotal in your journey toward financial freedom.

Why It Matters:

- Holding onto past financial mistakes or regrets can hinder progress and perpetuate negative beliefs.

- Self-forgiveness is a crucial element of healing, allowing you to let go of guilt and shame.

The Process:

- Acknowledge past financial mistakes without self-judgment.

- Understand that everyone makes financial errors, and it's a part of the learning process.

- Practice self-compassion and replace self-blame with self-acceptance.

The Power of Self-Forgiveness: Forgiving yourself liberates you from the weight of past financial missteps, enabling a fresh start. It fosters self-compassion, reduces the emotional burden associated with money-block issues, and paves the way for healthier financial decisions. Self-forgiveness is a critical component of building a positive relationship with money.

Step 4: Rethink Your Money Belief

This step marks a turning point in your journey towards overcoming money block issues. It's all about reevaluating and reshaping your deeply ingrained beliefs about money.

Why It Matters:

- Your money beliefs often drive your financial decisions and behaviors.

- By reevaluating and altering these beliefs, you can align them with your financial goals and aspirations.

The Process:

- Begin by identifying your negative money beliefs. For example, "I'll never be financially secure."

- Challenge the validity of this belief. Ask yourself if there's any concrete evidence supporting it.

- Replace the negative belief with a more positive and empowering one. In this case, "I am capable of achieving financial security through careful planning and effort."

- Continuously reinforce this positive belief through affirmations and actions.

The Power of Transforming Your Money Belief: By altering your money belief, you change the narrative you've been telling yourself about your financial situation. It's a profound shift that can reshape your financial decisions and ultimately lead you toward financial freedom. The process of transformation isn't just about thinking differently; it's about acting in alignment with your newly cultivated positive beliefs. This step holds the potential to be the cornerstone of your financial transformation, enabling you to make more informed and empowered financial decisions that better align with your goals and values.

Step 5: Gain Clarity

In Step 5, we delve into the importance of gaining clarity in your financial journey. Clarity is like a compass guiding you toward your financial goals and aspirations.

Why It Matters:

- Without a clear vision of your financial objectives, you may drift aimlessly.
- Clarity empowers you to set concrete goals and develop a strategic financial plan.

The Process:

- Start by defining your short-term and long-term financial goals. These might include saving for a home, retirement, education, or a dream vacation.
- Create a budget that outlines your income, expenses, and savings goals. This provides a clear snapshot of your financial landscape.
- Prioritize your goals, determining which are most important to you and which can be achieved in the short term.
- Break down larger goals into manageable steps. For instance, if you're saving for a house, set milestones for saving the down payment.
- Regularly review and adjust your financial plan as your circumstances change.

The Power of Gaining Clarity: Clarity brings your financial objectives into focus, providing you with a roadmap to guide your financial decisions. It helps you distinguish between essential expenses and discretionary spending, ensuring that your money is channeled toward your priorities. As you gain clarity, your financial journey becomes more purposeful and fulfilling, and you're better equipped to make decisions that align with your vision for a secure and prosperous future. This step is integral in helping you create a stable financial foundation.

Step 6: Be Proud

You've come a long way, and it's taken a good deal of introspection and confronting your own limitations and misconceptions to break through those barriers. This process of self-discovery can be tough, but it's a crucial step towards improving yourself and nurturing a more harmonious relationship with your partner when it comes to managing money. Kudos to you for taking these challenging steps.

Some of the steps we've discussed may require involving your partner. For instance, in step 5, "Gaining Clarity," you'll need to define your short and long-term financial goals and establish their priority. In any committed relationship, it's best to collaborate with your partner on matters like these. However, the initial steps can be embarked upon independently.

It's essential to remember that you need to be a mentally healthy individual before you can contribute to a healthy relationship. These efforts you're making for your own well-being will ultimately benefit your partnership.

Three Essential Financial Discussions for You and Your Partner

If you have one main takeaway from this entire book, it's this: It's essential for you and your partner to have the three crucial money conversations we're about to discuss. These discussions are the foundation of a healthy financial relationship and can help you align your financial values, prioritize your goals, and ensure a harmonious approach to managing your finances together. By engaging in open and honest conversations about money, you can strengthen your partnership and work towards shared financial success. Let's dive into these three key discussions that will set you on the path to financial well-being (Trantham, 2018):

The "This Is What My Money Looks Like" Conversation

When you aim to foster a healthy financial relationship with your partner, secrecy is simply not an option. That's because when you and your partner don't clearly understand each other's financial situations, it becomes nearly impossible to map out a joint plan for your financial future. The first and most crucial step is to open up about where you each stand financially.

This conversation is about transparency and vulnerability. It's an opportunity to lay all your financial cards on the table. Start by sharing your income, expenses, debts, savings, and financial goals. Be honest about your financial strengths and any challenges you may be facing.

Why is this conversation so important? Firstly, it builds trust. It shows that you are willing to be open and honest about your financial circumstances. It's a way of saying, "I trust you with my financial truth, and I want us to work together to create a more secure financial future."

Secondly, it forms the foundation for your financial plan. With a comprehensive understanding of each other's financial positions, you can set realistic goals, create a budget that works for both of you, and determine how you will approach shared expenses and savings.

This discussion may not always be easy. It can be uncomfortable to reveal financial difficulties or debts, but addressing them and working together toward solutions is essential. Remember that you're a team, and by sharing your financial reality, you can navigate the ups and downs of life as a united front. Openness and transparency in this conversation can set the stage for financial success and ensure that both you and your partner are on the same page as you build a secure and fulfilling financial future together.

The "What Are Our Money Goals?" Conversation

Your financial future as a couple begins with this pivotal conversation. It's here that you lay the foundation for your shared financial dreams. At first, your money goals may not align perfectly, and that's perfectly normal. However, with open communication and a willingness to compromise from both parties, you can work towards a common financial vision or find ways to navigate your key differences.

In this conversation, you explore your individual aspirations and financial objectives. What financial objectives do you have in both the near and distant future? What are your dreams and ambitions for your life together? Do you want to buy a home, travel the world, start a family, or save for early retirement?

While your goals might not be identical, it's essential to understand each other's priorities and values. For instance, one of you may prioritize saving for a stress-free retirement, while the other values investing in your children's education. Through open and empathetic communication, you can find ways to compromise, create a shared set of financial goals, and develop a plan to achieve them together.

This conversation is a cornerstone of your financial partnership. It not only helps you set financial objectives but also deepens your understanding of each other's hopes and dreams. Discussing and aligning your money goals will strengthen your relationship, build a unified financial plan, and ensure that your financial decisions are in harmony with your shared vision for a prosperous future.

The "How Are We Going to Combine Finances?" Conversation

As you embark on your financial journey together, one of the key discussions you'll need to have is about how you'll manage your finances as a couple. This conversation revolves around finding a financial structure that works for both of you.

Depending on your and your partner's preferences and styles, you may choose to have a joint bank account, maintain individual accounts, or strike a balance between the two. Importantly, there's no one-size-fits-all solution here. What matters most is finding an approach that suits both of you and aligns with your shared financial goals.

This conversation involves discussing how you'll handle income, expenses, savings, and investments as a couple. Are you comfortable with pooling all your finances into a joint account? Or do you prefer to keep some financial independence by maintaining separate accounts while contributing to shared expenses and savings? (See Chapter 7 for a deep dive into the pros and cons of these different options.)

The key to this conversation is understanding each other's financial expectations and finding common ground. It's essential to discuss how you'll manage your everyday expenses, how you'll save for your goals, and how you'll make financial decisions together. By openly communicating about this, you can avoid misunderstandings and ensure that your financial structure supports your shared objectives.

Keep in mind that there is no universally applicable method for handling finances as a couple. What's most important is that you and your partner find a solution that works for your unique relationship and financial circumstances. In this conversation, you'll define the financial path that best suits both of you, creating a framework for managing your finances harmoniously as a team.

Five Simple Steps to Get on the Same Page Financially with Your Partner

Indeed, differences are inevitable, but finding common ground goes a long way in maintaining a harmonious financial partnership with your spouse. Here are five straightforward steps to help you and your spouse get on the same page financially:

Open the Lines of Communication

Yes, open communication keeps coming up. That's because a strong, honest dialogue can eliminate misunderstandings and build a solid financial partnership.

Define Your Shared Goals

Take time to sit down together and identify your shared financial goals. Discuss what you want to achieve as a couple – whether it's buying a home, saving for your children's education, or planning for retirement. Setting common objectives gives you a clear direction for your financial decisions and a sense of purpose in managing your money.

Create a Budget Together

A budget is your roadmap to financial success. Work together to create a budget that outlines your income, expenses, savings, and debt repayment plans. This joint effort allows you to allocate resources efficiently and ensures that your financial choices are aligned with your shared goals.

Decide on Financial Roles

Consider defining your financial roles within the relationship. Discuss who will manage bills, monitor investments, or handle other financial responsibilities. Clarity in these roles can prevent misunderstandings and ensure that both partners contribute to the family's economic well-being.

Regularly Review and Adjust

Life is constantly changing, just like your financial situation. Make it a habit to review your financial plan regularly. Discuss any changes in your goals, income, or expenses. This periodic evaluation ensures that your financial strategy remains relevant and adaptable to the evolving needs of your partnership.

By taking these simple yet impactful steps, you and your spouse can bridge the gap in your financial approaches and cultivate a strong, shared financial future. Remember that your financial journey is a collaborative effort, and by working together, you can overcome differences and create a harmonious, prosperous life together.

Providing Strategies for Addressing and Overcoming Financial Fears in a Partnership

No relationship is immune to occasional money problems and disagreements. For some couples, these financial conflicts have even become the norm. But what if I told you there are straightforward strategies that can help you not only overcome these issues but also reduce their frequency? In this section, we'll explore practical solutions to address and conquer financial fears within a partnership (Davis, 2022):

Build a Foundation of Honesty and Trust

As per insights from experts, the initial and crucial step in addressing financial issues in a relationship is to establish open and honest communication. Renowned relationship coach John Kenny underscores the pivotal role of trust in this process (Davis, 2022). Kenny emphasizes that while it's not necessary to discuss every single purchase with your partner, maintaining financial secrecy or making significant decisions unilaterally can lead to relationship impasses or disagreements.

Kenny further suggests that discussing your respective perspectives on money is vital. This involves delving into your beliefs, fears, and the role of money in your lives, as we did in Chapters 1 and 2. Once you understand each other's financial mindsets, communication can flow more freely.

Despite the apparent simplicity of these steps, many individuals find money-related conversations highly charged and challenging. Surprisingly, research reveals that a significant 39% of adults avoid discussing money with their partners. Even though a substantial 58% of us acknowledge that dishonesty about money could lead to the end of a relationship, these discussions often remain elusive.

Use supportive language

While being open and honest with your partner about financial concerns is crucial, it's equally important to approach these discussions with care and empathy rather than assigning blame, especially if you believe your partner needs to change certain habits. Instead, aim to establish a supportive and understanding connection. This approach can significantly reduce stress levels in various high-pressure situations.

Dr. Touroni, a renowned expert in relationship dynamics, emphasizes the significance of the language you use during these conversations (Davis, 2022). She advises against employing blaming language, such as phrases like "you spend too much" or using extreme terms like "always" and "never," which can be inflammatory and counterproductive. Criticism and blame have detrimental consequences in the context of a relationship.

Instead, focus on using "I" statements when discussing financial matters. For instance, you can express your feelings by saying, "I feel concerned about our current spending habits" or "I'd like us to have a conversation about our finances." This approach places the emphasis on your emotions and concerns, making it less likely to trigger a defensive or negative reaction in your partner.

Budget Together

Financial experts often stress the importance of evaluating your financial situation, establishing clear goals, and devising a budget. While the prospect of budgeting may appear daunting, numerous budget planning tools are available to simplify the process. (See Chapter 7 for a list of top budgeting websites and apps.)

For couples, especially those in long-term or married relationships, approaching this task as a team can be a healthy and constructive strategy. To alleviate potential stress and maintain a relaxed atmosphere during financial discussions, consider choosing a casual setting, like your favorite coffee shop.

One effective approach to reframing the conversation is to center it around short and long-term financial goals. Doing so can transform a potentially negative and stressful topic into a more positive one. While money-related issues might occasionally dampen the joy in your relationship, setting and working toward common goals can rekindle your shared enthusiasm for the exciting milestones you aim to achieve together.

Make Time for Fun

Dr. Touroni offers valuable advice, emphasizing the importance of allocating time for activities that bring you and your partner closer and promote a sense of enjoyment and well-being. This becomes even more critical during challenging periods of a relationship (Davis, 2022).

Regrettably, when grappling with low self-esteem and stress stemming from financial issues, it can be easy to convince ourselves that we can't afford or perhaps don't deserve to partake in enjoyable moments with our partners. However, prioritizing these shared experiences is incredibly beneficial, both for your personal well-being and the health of your relationship.

Fortunately, there is a multitude of cost-effective or even free activities that couples can relish together, including:

- nature walks and picnics
- bicycle outings
- themed movie nights

- exploring nearby no-cost attractions such as art galleries, castles, and museums

- preparing a new meal together

- engaging in sports games at a local park

- creating photo albums filled with cherished memories.

Through engaging in these fun activities, you and your partner can remember to cherish the simple joys of togetherness.

Take One Day at a Time

Once you've reinforced the idea that you and your partner are tackling financial challenges as a united front, it's beneficial to maintain a focus on the present moment. Dr. Touroni recommends taking life one day at a time and refraining from excessive predictions about the future or dwelling on the most pessimistic scenarios. Instead, direct your attention toward what you can manage in the present and do so together.

This mindfulness practice involves anchoring your thoughts in the current moment. Research has revealed that mindfulness can be a valuable tool for soothing emotional turmoil and enhancing self-compassion (Davis, 2022). By embracing this approach, you and your partner can navigate financial hardships with greater resilience and mutual support.

♥ • $ • ♥ • $ • ♥

In Chapter 3, you broke down the walls that hinder financial bliss in your relationship. Here are the highlights:

- **Personal Barriers:** Your upbringing and past experiences can create financial tension in your relationship.

- **Money Obstacles**: Identifying your money obstacles is the first step to overcoming limiting beliefs.

- **Silly Interrupters:** Playful tactics challenge negative beliefs and encourage self-reflection.

- **Contradictory Proof**: Seek evidence that challenges limiting money beliefs for a healthier financial mindset.

- **Self-Forgiveness**: Forgiving yourself for past financial mistakes fosters self-compassion.

- **Rethinking Money Beliefs:** Reshape ingrained money beliefs to make better financial decisions.

- **Gaining Clarity**: Set clear financial objectives, create budgets, prioritize goals, and break them into manageable steps.

- **Taking Pride in Progress**: Celebrate your journey to improve your financial mindset.

- **Three Essential Financial Discussions**: Discuss your current finances, money goals, and how to combine finances.

- **Five Simple Steps for Financial Alignment**: Communicate openly, set shared goals, budget together, define financial roles, and regularly review your plan.

- **Strategies for Addressing Financial Fears**: Build trust, use supportive language, budget as a team, make finances fun, and take it one step at a time.

Chapter 3 was quite an adventure, both in writing and learning. I found it so enlightening that I've decided to dust off the ol' financial discussion playbook.

You see, my partner isn't exactly thrilled when I spring these talks on him. So, I've devised a brilliant plan – I'm scheduling a meeting and luring him in with the promise of a delicious home-cooked meal. Classic bribery, right?

But let's get back to the main course, Chapter 3. It's like a treasure map to financial bliss, guiding us through open communication, shared goals, and the power of teamwork. So, whether you're discussing money over dinner or devising a grand financial plan, this chapter's got your back.

Make a difference in 60 seconds by reviewing this book!

Your review can inspire other couples to take the first step towards financial success!

The Romance of Wealth – Personal Finance for Couples aims to empower its readers to take the reins of their finances. As you celebrate the milestones in your financial journey together, why not share your joy and learning with others? Your review of our book can be a valuable source of encouragement and guidance for couples just starting out or those facing financial hurdles. Tell us how our book helped in shaping your financial strategies and relationship goals. Your story can make a difference!

https://bit.ly/review4love

Maria and Jack's Story

In the serene suburb of Willow Creek, there lived a couple, Maria and Jack, whose love was as deep as the ocean but still often found themselves navigating the choppy waters of financial disagreement. Maria was the breadwinner of the family, her career in software development blossoming, while Jack, a freelance photographer, contributed inconsistently due to the nature of his work.

One evening, as the golden hues of sunset bathed their home, a tension-filled silence replaced their usual banter. Maria had discovered that Jack, swayed by his passion for vintage camera gear, had once again overshot their carefully planned budget. The purchase, though beautiful, was impractical, and it stung Maria's sense of financial responsibility.

"Again, Jack?" Maria's voice was a mixture of disappointment and fatigue, echoing off the walls of their otherwise tranquil home. "We have goals, savings, we talked about this..."

Jack's defense was passionate, his belief that life was too short to not pursue one's passions. But in his heart, he knew he had crossed a line. The camera was not just an object of desire; it had become a symbol of their recurring conflict.

The night was long, the air charged with arguments about money, respect, and partnership. They grappled with the imbalance, the unspoken fears that money, the fuel of their lives, could also be the wedge that drove them apart.

It took many such nights, but eventually, Maria and Jack found their middle ground. They sought the counsel of a financial advisor and attended workshops, learning to communicate their fears and understand each other's values. They established a discretionary fund for Jack's occasional splurges and reinforced their shared goals with renewed commitment.

MARIA AND JACK'S STORY

Over time, they learned that their love was not measured by the money they made or spent but by their willingness to bridge their differences and work as a team.

Chapter 4

Communication About Money: How to Talk About Money Without Fighting or Shaming

In this chapter, we further embark on a journey towards mastering the art of financial communication within your relationship. Our aim is to help couples not only talk about money but also do so without fear of arguments or judgment. By understanding each other's unique financial perspectives, finding common ground, and fostering empathy in your discussions about money, you can cultivate the kind of financial compatibility that leads to harmony and understanding.

Imagine a scenario where you and your partner can openly converse about financial matters, sharing your thoughts, concerns, and aspirations, knowing that you are both on the same page. What if these discussions could bring you closer rather than drive a wedge between you? This chapter is your guide to making these aspirations a reality. Let's explore the art of building financial compatibility together.

Fostering Financial Harmony Through Understanding Perspectives

We've already learned that how you and your partner perceive and approach money topics significantly influences your decisions together. This understanding goes beyond the mere acknowledgment of your partner's financial habits; it delves into the deeper layers of their beliefs, fears, and values related to money.

By gaining insight into each other's financial perspectives, you can navigate your financial discussions with greater empathy and sensitivity. Let's dig deeper into why this matters:

Enhanced Empathy: When you understand your partner's financial perspective, you can better appreciate their financial decisions, even if they differ from your own. This empathy is the cornerstone of productive financial discussions, as it prevents judgment and criticism.

Informed Decision-Making: Your partner's financial perspective might shed light on why they prioritize certain expenses or savings goals. Understanding these motivations can help both of you make more informed and mutually agreeable financial choices.

Conflict Resolution: Disagreements about money are a common source of relationship conflict. However, understanding each other's financial perspectives makes you better able to resolve conflicts amicably. You can address the root causes of financial disagreements and work towards mutually satisfying solutions.

Building a Shared Financial Vision: As you comprehend each other's financial perspectives, you can begin to construct a shared financial vision that takes into account both partners' values and goals. This shared vision becomes a unifying force, steering your financial decisions in a direction that aligns with your collective aspirations.

In essence, understanding your partner's financial perspective is about more than just acknowledging their financial habits; it's about gaining a deep comprehension of their relationship with money. This understanding can foster empathy, enhance your decision-making process, and lay the groundwork for resolving conflicts and building a prosperous financial future together. It's a key component of financial compatibility and the foundation for fruitful financial discussions.

Effective Strategies for Sharing Your Financial Perspective

What if you could make the process of discussing finances with your partner not only productive but enjoyable, too? While financial conversations can sometimes feel daunting, there's no reason they can't also be fun, romantic, and filled with learning opportunities. One creative approach is to schedule a financial date night, where you and your partner can navigate money discussions with ease (Marter, 2022).

Why Financial Date Nights Matter

Financial date nights offer numerous benefits in the realm of financial discussions:

Creating an Open Environment: During a date night, you're more likely to approach the conversation with an open mind, ready to hear each other's perspectives and share your own. It sets a positive tone for the discussion.

Encouraging Assertiveness: A date night can empower you to assertively express your thoughts and feelings about money without fear of judgment. It's a platform for you and your partner to speak your mind.

Taking It Step by Step: To avoid feeling overwhelmed, financial date nights allow you to take baby steps in your discussions. You can focus on one aspect of your finances at a time, making the process more manageable.

Learning and Growing Together: Sharing financial insights and knowledge can become a learning experience for both you and your partner. It's an opportunity to grow together and strengthen your financial compatibility.

How to Make it Work:

- **Setting the Scene:** Choose a comfortable setting that appeals to both of you, whether it's a cozy corner of your home, a favorite restaurant, or a tranquil outdoor spot.

- **Establish an Agenda:** Outline the topics you'd like to cover during your financial date night. Prioritize what's most important to you and take it one step at a time. Don't try to cover all the important topics at once.

- **Maintain a Positive Atmosphere**: Keep the discussion positive and non-judgmental. Remember, the goal is to work together toward your financial goals and aspirations. No shaming or blaming.

- **Share Knowledge:** Use this time to express your views and share your financial knowledge. Teach each other, learn together, and grow as a couple.

Financial date nights are a creative and constructive way to enhance financial communication. By fostering an environment of openness, assertiveness, and learning, you can transform money discussions from daunting to delightful. So, why not infuse your financial talks with the spirit of romance and growth?

Active Listening: A Key to Understanding in Financial Conversations

Yes, you can set a romantic mood to discuss finances with your partner, but here's the catch: if you're not displaying the signs of an active listener, the romance might quickly evaporate. Nobody wants to feel like their opinions don't matter, and using such an approach can lead to relationship turbulence rather than harmony. That's where the art of active listening comes into play. It's a key element that can transform your financial conversations.

Active listening is not just about hearing; it's about understanding and empathizing with your partner's perspective. In this section, we'll delve into the significance of active listening in financial discussions and explore practical techniques to make your partner feel heard and valued in these important conversations. It's a skill that can bring you closer and build trust in your financial partnership. Active listening skills include (Wooll, 2022):

Providing Eye Contact

While it might initially seem daunting, maintaining eye contact in a conversation, especially during financial discussions with your partner, offers substantial advantages. This practice taps into our brain's limbic mirror system, fostering a deeper level of understanding between individuals. Essentially, when we look into someone's eyes, our brains mirror the neurons firing in their brain, establishing a unique connection.

This visual connection can significantly impact the emotional dynamics of a conversation. If your partner's eyes convey contentment, you will also likely feel content. Similarly, if they express sadness or concern, you'll naturally empathize and share those emotions. By engaging in active listening with a focus on eye contact, you and your partner can forge a stronger connection and deepen your mutual empathy. It's a non-verbal form of communication that can enhance your financial discussions and foster a closer, more harmonious financial partnership.

Asking Questions

Engaging in active listening through the art of asking thoughtful questions is a powerful tool for understanding your partner's financial perspective. This practice not only signifies your sincere interest in their viewpoint but also generates detailed, meaningful responses. Open-ended questions, in particular, facilitate in-depth discussions, steering clear of one-word answers that can stifle communication.

Various types of questions serve distinct purposes, such as problem-solving, guiding the conversation's flow, or achieving closure. Incorporating questions like "What concerns you most about this situation?" or "How do you envision improvements with more time?" helps unearth deeper insights and emotions, fostering a stronger connection and empathy. These questions become invaluable assets in enhancing your financial discussions and nurturing a more profound comprehension of your partner's financial viewpoint.

Paying Attention to Non-Verbal Cues

Mastering the art of reading nonverbal cues like body language, voice tone, eye contact, and facial expressions is a pivotal skill in deciphering the subtler aspects of a conversation. These cues provide valuable insights into the emotions and unspoken sentiments of those we engage with. By honing this ability, we can adapt our approach to diffuse hostility, comfort someone's nervousness, or offer support to uplift their spirits. Moreover, our attentive and open nonverbal signals indicate that we are actively and empathetically listening to our conversation partners, fostering a deeper and more meaningful connection.

Steering Clear of Judgment

Engaging in non-judgmental active listening is a powerful tool for building empathy and creating a safe space for open communication. When we approach conversations without preconceived judgments or biases, we leave room for understanding and connection. Maintaining an open mind and fostering compassion are essential components of this approach, as they help the other person feel heard and validated in their thoughts and feelings.

Avoid Interrupting Your Partner

Prioritizing active listening over excessive talking demonstrates our commitment to being present in the conversation rather than getting lost in self-centered thoughts. It's a way of giving the other person the space they need to think and share without interruptions.

In these moments, exercising patience and allowing your partner to complete their thoughts is crucial. This holds even more significance when tackling complex issues, as it ensures you gather all the pertinent information before attempting to solve problems or provide insights. Listening with patience is the foundation of constructive and effective communication.

Paraphrasing

Active listening becomes particularly important in romantic relationships, and summarizing your partner's words with thoughtful questions can enhance your connection. For instance, you could say, "So, if I understand correctly, spending more quality time together would make you feel more cherished?" or "Am I right in thinking that you'd appreciate it if I checked in with you more during the day?" These questions express your commitment to understanding and nurturing your romantic connection, fostering empathy and harmony in your relationship.

Sharing Similar Experiences

Sharing similar life experiences can be a powerful way to foster vulnerability and compassion, ultimately forging a deeper connection with others. When individuals find common ground through shared experiences, they tend to feel less judged and more inclined to trust one another. However, it's crucial to ensure that when sharing a personal story to relate to someone, you don't inadvertently steer the conversation towards yourself. The key is to use your experience to empathize with their situation and then pivot the discussion back to them.

For example, you may say something like:

- "I know how stressful managing finances can be, especially when we're planning for our future together. When I was saving for a down payment on our home, it seemed daunting. Let's work together to make our financial goals a reality."

- "I've been through the process of paying off student loans, so I understand how it can weigh on your mind. We can create a strategy to tackle it together and secure a debt-free future."

- "Balancing a budget isn't always easy, but I've been there too. When we talk about our financial goals, remember that we're in this together, and I'm here to support our aspirations."

In these examples, your shared financial experiences can alleviate your partner's stress and build trust. They'll feel reassured that you understand their financial concerns and are committed to achieving your goals together.

Providing Feedback

Giving verbal feedback is a simple yet effective way to demonstrate active listening and genuine empathy. When your partner shares their joys, expressing enthusiasm and support, like saying, "That's wonderful news, you truly deserve it!" can reinforce their positive emotions. Conversely, when they open up about challenges, acknowledging their difficulties with responses such as "That must be incredibly tough" or "I can't imagine how heavy that experience must be" conveys your understanding and compassion.

This verbal feedback not only validates their emotions but also strengthens your connection by showing that you're fully present and engaged in the conversation. It's a way to let them know you're there to share in their joy or provide support during their struggles.

♥ · $ · ♥ · $ · ♥

Chapter 4 focused on improving financial communication. It highlights the significance of understanding each other's financial perspectives, embracing empathy, and creating an environment of harmonious financial discussions. The key takeaways from this chapter are as follows:

- **Understanding Financial Perspectives:** Gain insight into your partner's financial perspective, delving into their beliefs, fears, and values related to money. This deeper understanding fosters empathy and informed decision-making.

- **Fostering Empathy:** Understanding your partner's financial perspective allows you to empathize with their financial decisions, reducing judgment and criticism. This empathy is essential for productive financial discussions.

- **Conflict Resolution:** With a deep understanding of your partner's financial viewpoint, you can address the root causes of financial disagreements and work towards mutually satisfying solutions. This paves the way for resolving conflicts amicably.

- **Building a Shared Financial Vision:** Comprehending each other's financial perspectives enables you to construct a shared financial vision that aligns with your collective values and goals. This shared vision guides your financial decisions toward your aspirations.

- **Financial Date Nights:** Experiment with the concept of financial date nights, where you and your partner can engage in open and productive financial discussions. This approach sets a positive tone, encourages assertiveness, and promotes learning and growth.

- **Active Listening:** Active listening is a key element in financial conversations. Techniques include maintaining eye contact, asking questions, paying attention to non-verbal cues, avoiding judgment, refraining from interrupting, paraphrasing, sharing similar experiences, and providing feedback.

These strategies aim to make financial discussions enjoyable and constructive while strengthening the emotional connection between partners. Active listening, in particular, is highlighted as a crucial skill for understanding and empathizing with your partner's financial perspective. The skills you've learned in this chapter create a safe space for open communication and mutual understanding and build a bedrock of trust that allows you to take the next step in creating a harmonious financial partnership.

Samantha and Alex's Story

Samantha and Alex had always prided themselves on being a team, but as they navigated the demanding currents of middle age, they found themselves at a crossroads that neither foresaw. With two bright children ready to embark on their educational journeys and Alex's mother requiring more care than they could provide, their once-aligned priorities began to diverge sharply.

Alex was adamant that his mother, who had single-handedly raised him, deserved the comfort and dignity of a top-tier assisted living facility. He envisioned a place where she would receive the care she needed, with facilities that felt like a continuation of her own home.

Samantha, on the other hand, was equally passionate about investing in their children's future. The local public schools were good, but the private schools—with their stellar resources and track records of success—seemed like a golden ticket to the best universities and a secure future.

Each night, their conversations spiraled into a loop of "What about the kids?" and "What about mom?" The tension was palpable, their dinner table no longer a place of communal solace but a battleground for conflicting loyalties. They both lay awake at night, wondering if their inability to agree on where to allocate their finances was a sign of a deeper incompatibility.

The idea of divorce, once unthinkable, now crept into their exhausted minds. Could a partnership survive such fundamental discord? Yet, amidst the turmoil, their love—a love that had once felt invincible—now seemed to be the only glue keeping them together.

It was during a particularly silent car ride home from visiting a private school that Samantha reached for Alex's hand. "We can't let this break us," she whispered.

The breakthrough came when they sought the counsel of a financial planner, who helped them explore options they hadn't considered—scholarships, alternative care

SAMANTHA AND ALEX'S STORY

solutions, and a reevaluation of their assets and budget. It was painstaking work, filled with compromise and sacrifice, but it was work they did together.

They found a middle ground, choosing a more affordable care facility for Alex's mother that offered quality care and a charter school with a robust program for their children. The solution wasn't perfect, but it was a plan that honored both of their values.

With time, the tension eased. They learned that love wasn't just about sharing dreams but also about shouldering each other's deepest concerns. As they navigated this challenging chapter, their respect for one another grew, and so did their understanding that compatibility isn't about never disagreeing; it's about finding a way forward together.

Chapter 5

United We Stand: Aligning Your Financial Priorities

As mentioned earlier, I'm sticking to my commitment to make your reading experience as smooth as possible. Brace yourself because this is one of those chapters that is so full of financial bundles of insight that I've thoughtfully divided it into sections.

In previous chapters, we delved into the pivotal aspects of achieving financial harmony in your relationship. We shed light on how building a solid financial future together necessitates aligning your financial goals and comprehending each other's unique perspectives. It's my hope that through gaining these essential insights, you'll obtain the tools necessary for shaping a shared financial vision that will guide your journey as a couple.

In this chapter, we will navigate through the critical elements of this financial partnership (what it really entails and how to navigate it harmoniously). With that in mind, please keep the following example in mind to see how sweeping things under the carpet or putting off important conversations can affect the dynamics of your relationship:

Nick and Jennifer

The two met and fell in love five years ago. She is a lawyer for a charity, and he practices law in court. They tied the knot in 2017 and welcomed a child the following year. Jennifer wanted to become a stay-at-home mom after the birth of her child. That had always been the plan in her head. She had a respectable income, though it was not nearly as high as her husband's.

They were comfortable financially and didn't need the extra money, so remaining at home made sense. Jennifer reasoned that not only would they save money by not having to pay for childcare, clothing, dry cleaning, gas, lunches, and so on, but she would also get to be the primary caregiver for their child rather than handing that position over to a complete stranger.

To her dismay, Jennifer found that Nick had no idea what she was planning until she told him. Why? Simply put, they never took the time to plan ahead and talk about it. Nick simply assumed that after having a child, Jennifer would go back to work. He believed that they could afford to hire a babysitter and, more importantly, had become accustomed to the comfortable lifestyle that their two paychecks allowed them to maintain. After the birth of their child, Nick and Jennifer had different visions of what their future should hold. They had divergent opinions on how much money was "enough" and whether or not they could get by on only one income.

Situations like the one experienced by Nick and Jennifer are not uncommon in relationships. Many of us have found ourselves in situations where conflicting views about money, both in the present and the future, arise with our partners. Sometimes, we avoid discussing these issues because we assume that our perspective is the most logical or natural one. But is that assumption always accurate? As we reflect on this, let's consider the following questions:

- How can my partner and I ensure that we're aligning our financial goals and expectations early in our relationship to avoid misunderstandings like the one between Nick and Jennifer?

- What strategies can we use to effectively communicate our financial expectations and long-term plans, especially when it comes to significant life events such as having children, their college funds, joint investments, debt, and retirement goals?

- How can we balance our desire for a comfortable lifestyle with the financial flexibility needed to adapt to changing circumstances, such as a partner wanting to become a stay-at-home parent?

- How can we navigate differences in income and financial priorities to ensure we both feel valued and understood in the partnership?

- What strategies or tools can we use to create a shared financial vision that accommodates our individual perspectives and helps us plan for a successful financial future together?

There's certainly a lot to delve into here, isn't there? I have a deep passion for relationships, harmony, and financial stability, and I'm genuinely excited about the insights we can gain from this pivotal chapter. My hope is that we'll all discover something profoundly meaningful in the pages that follow.

Section 1: Investment Styles and Strategies

Within the realm of financial alignment, being familiar with various investment approaches allows you and your partner to identify the strategies that resonate with your shared goals, risk tolerance, and economic aspirations.

This knowledge not only facilitates more confident financial choices but also fosters unity in financial planning, ensuring that both you and your partner are on the same page and working together towards your financial objectives. In the following sections, we will explore the intricacies of investment styles and how they can be tailored to suit your unique financial partnership.

Understanding Investment Approaches

An investing style is a guide that helps people decide how to invest their money. It considers things like how much risk they're comfortable with, how long they want to invest, and their personal values. Some styles take more risks for the chance of making more money.

If someone doesn't have the time or knowledge to manage their investments, they can pay a professional to do it for them in something called a managed account.

It's important to avoid common mistakes like making impulsive or emotional investments or trading stocks frequently. Regardless of the chosen style, people should always do their homework before making investment choices that fit their specific goals and situations.

What Is Risk Tolerance?

Risk tolerance is all about how comfortable you are with the idea that your investments may sometimes lose value. To determine your risk tolerance, think about how you'd feel if your investments dropped significantly when the stock market wasn't doing well.

There's a saying on Wall Street that goes, "You can eat well, or you can sleep well." Eating well means that, over a long time, taking more risks, like investing in stocks, can help you make a lot of money (McBride, 2023). But the catch is that stocks can be unpredictable and may cause some sleepless nights.

At the end of this Section, we've included a quiz that will help you determine your own and your partner's risk tolerance. Answer the questions honestly to gain insight into your comfort level with financial risk.

Why Does Risk Tolerance Matter?

Think of your risk tolerance as the foundation of your money-growing plan, allowing you to build wealth without constantly worrying about it. If the idea of your money's value going up and down, even for a short time, makes you uncomfortable, you might prefer safer investments that might not earn as much.

Investments with higher potential returns can also mean a greater chance of sudden drops or losses.

Once you know your risk tolerance, you can develop an investment strategy that balances your concerns about unpredictable changes with the potential for higher profits.

Here's how it works:

Evaluating your risk tolerance is essential, especially when the stock market takes a hit. Reflect on the events of March 2020, when the stock market experienced a sharp decline. Job losses were rampant, and the world faced unprecedented uncertainty due to the COVID-19 pandemic, which had the potential to wreck the economy.

Ask yourself, how did you handle it? Did you hold onto your investments through those turbulent times, or did you sell in a panic? If you held on, your risk tolerance was likely high. On the other hand, if you decided to sell amid the chaos, your risk tolerance may have been low.

Fast forward to 2021, and the stock market rebounded to record highs. If you had the courage to invest more during the market downturn, it suggests that your risk tolerance is on the higher side.

The year 2022 posed another test as interest rates rose, causing both stocks and bonds to decline. Some riskier stocks saw significant drops in value, leading to questions about company valuations and concerns about a potential recession (McBride, 2023).

Types of Risk Tolerance

To better comprehend your own or your partner's risk tolerance, it's beneficial to consider various risk tolerance profiles that individuals typically fall into.

These profiles help in understanding how comfortable one is with taking risks in one's investments. Here are the primary categories:

Conservative: A conservative risk tolerance profile indicates a preference for minimal risk. People with a conservative approach are more inclined to protect their investments and prioritize safety over higher returns. They often opt for low-risk, stable investments like bonds, certificates of deposit (CDs), or money market accounts. While this approach may provide a sense of security, it may also limit the potential for substantial wealth growth.

Moderate: A moderate risk tolerance suggests a balanced approach. Individuals with this profile are open to some level of risk to pursue moderate returns. They typically diversify their investments across a mix of asset classes, such as stocks and bonds, to balance growth potential and stability. This approach aims to capture the benefits of both safety and potential growth.

Aggressive: An aggressive risk tolerance profile reflects a willingness to embrace higher risk for the prospect of substantial returns. Individuals in this category are more comfortable with market volatility and are often drawn to investments with greater growth potential, such as individual stocks or high-risk/high-reward opportunities. While this approach can yield significant profits, it also exposes investments to higher levels of market fluctuation.

It's important to note that these risk tolerance profiles are not set in stone and can evolve based on financial goals, life circumstances, and market conditions. A healthy financial partnership involves open communication to ensure that both partners are on the same page regarding their risk tolerance and investment choices, allowing for a balanced and aligned approach to managing money.

How to Determine Your Risk Tolerance

You can answer these crucial questions to determine your risk tolerance (McBride, 2023):

What are my Investment Objectives? Your investment goals play a pivotal role in determining your risk tolerance. Ask yourself, what do I want to achieve with my investments? Am I constantly investing to build my wealth, or do I already have a substantial nest egg and aim to maintain it while relying on the income it generates?

These objectives lead to distinct preferences for dealing with potential losses in investment value. Your approach to risk will be influenced by whether your focus is on growth or preservation, highlighting the importance of aligning your financial strategy with your long-term goals.

When Do I Need the Money? The timing of when you'll require the money is a critical factor in determining your risk tolerance. Your investment horizon, or how long you have before needing the funds, significantly impacts your comfort level with risk. If you anticipate needing the money in the near future, like for a home down payment next year, your risk tolerance tends to be lower. In contrast, funds earmarked for retirement, which is several years down the road, come with a different time horizon, affording you a potentially higher risk tolerance as you have more time to ride out market fluctuations and pursue long-term growth.

What if I lose a Significant Percentage of My Investment this Year? Evaluating your risk tolerance includes considering how you would respond to potential setbacks and difficult situations. For instance, if your investment portfolio experienced a 20 percent decline in value during a year, would you find it distressing and decide to withdraw all your investments? Alternatively, would you keep your investments in place and perhaps even consider adding more money to benefit from the market's discounted prices? These hypothetical scenarios help you gauge your comfort level with risk and how you'd react under adverse conditions.

The Bottomline

These questions not only provide valuable insights into your own risk tolerance but also serve as an excellent starting point for understanding your partner's financial preferences and risk capacity. By openly discussing these scenarios and considerations, you can foster a constructive dialogue about your respective approaches to investing and finance.

This shared understanding can be the foundation for reaching a mutual compromise and aligning your financial goals and strategies, ensuring that both partners are comfortable with the investment choices made as a couple. This alignment not only helps manage risk but also strengthens the financial partnership, promoting trust and unity in your journey toward shared financial objectives.

Activity: Risk Tolerance Quiz

Individually, take the quiz included here. Add up your scores and then compare where each of you falls on the risk spectrum.

Questions:

When you hear the word "risk" in a financial context, which word comes closest to your initial feeling?
A. Anxiety (1 point)
B. Caution (2 points)
C. Necessity (3 points)
D. Opportunity (4 points)
E. Excitement (5 points)

How do you feel about the idea of investing in a new business venture?
A. Very uncomfortable (1 point)
B. Somewhat uncomfortable (2 points)
C. Neutral (3 points)

D. Somewhat comfortable (4 points)
E. Very comfortable (5 points)

Imagine you've received a significant sum of money. What would you most likely do with it?
A. Put it in a savings account (1 point)
B. Buy bonds or conservative funds (2 points)
C. Invest in a mix of stocks and bonds (3 points)
D. Invest mostly in stocks (4 points)
E. Invest in high-risk, high-reward options (5 points)

When considering a financial decision, which factor weighs more heavily on your mind?
A. The possibility of losing money (1 point)
B. The potential for a little growth with little risk (2 points)
C. A balance between growth potential and risk (3 points)
D. The potential for growth, even with some risk (4 points)
E. The chance to maximize returns, regardless of risk (5 points)

If you had to choose, which would you prefer?
A. A guaranteed small return (1 point)
B. A chance at a moderate return with some risk of loss (3 points)
C. A chance at a high return with a high risk of loss (5 points)

How do you usually make important financial decisions?
A. I avoid them as much as possible (1 point)
B. I take a lot of time to decide and often choose the safest option (2 points)
C. I seek advice from friends, family, or experts (3 points)
D. I consider the options and usually take a calculated risk (4 points)
E. I trust my gut and am not afraid to take risks (5 points)

When faced with a financial loss, what is your immediate reaction?
A. Panic and want to sell or move my money to a safer place (1 point)
B. Worry, but wait to see if the situation improves (2 points)

C. Monitor the situation, knowing these fluctuations are part of investing (3 points)

D. See it as a potential opportunity to invest more (4 points)

E. Get excited about the opportunity to "buy the dip" (5 points)

Results:

- **7-14 points:** Very Conservative - Prefers to avoid risks, values stability and predictability over potential gains.

- **15-21 points:** Conservative - Generally risk-averse but may be willing to take on a little risk for slightly higher returns.

- **22-28 points:** Moderate - Comfortable with a balanced approach to risk and returns.

- **29-35 points:** Aggressive - Willing to take on more risk for the possibility of higher returns.

- **36-42 points:** Very Aggressive - Embraces risk for the chance of significant gains and is not deterred by the possibility of losses.

Discussion questions:

- How has your risk tolerance been molded by your upbringing or experiences?

- How has your risk tolerance aided or hampered your overall financial position?

- Both ends of the risk spectrum have value. Is risk tolerance aligned between the two of us? If not, how can we both be more sensitive to each others' money comfort zone? Can these differences result in a healthy, balanced approach to financial decisions?

Section 2: Setting Joint Investment Goals

As I mentioned earlier, whether to have separate or joint accounts ultimately depends on your personal preferences as a couple. However, if you decide that a joint investment account is the path you'd like to explore, there are strategic ways to navigate this journey.

This section will delve into the art of setting joint investment goals. It's not just about merging finances; it's about aligning your aspirations, risk tolerance, and dreams to craft a shared vision for your financial future. We'll provide insights and tips on how to make this process both practical and rewarding so you and your partner can embark on this collaborative investment venture with confidence and unity. Let's take a look at these five crucial tips for investing jointly as a couple (Aditya et al., 2023):

Establish a Joint Investment Budget

Setting joint investment goals involves several key steps, including establishing a joint investment budget. To begin, merge your financial resources, taking into account your income and assets. Discuss your financial goals openly, as understanding your shared objectives is crucial. Assess your risk tolerance as a couple, ensuring that both partners are comfortable with the level of risk involved in your investments.

Craft an investment strategy that aligns with your goals and risk preferences, determining where you want to invest your funds and the appropriate asset allocation. Set a budget outlining how much you plan to invest regularly, whether it's a fixed amount or a percentage of your income. Periodically monitor and be prepared to adjust your joint investments as your goals and circumstances evolve. This process promotes transparency and teamwork and ensures that both partners actively contribute to their shared financial future.

Gain Insights into Each Other's Investment Styles

When it comes to setting joint investment goals, understanding each other's investor persona is a crucial step. This involves gaining insights into each partner's risk tolerance (as we've already discussed), investment time horizon, goals, preferred investment vehicles, involvement in decision-making, and communication methods.

By delving into these aspects, you can align your investment strategies with both partners' comfort levels and preferences, ensuring that your joint investment goals reflect a unified vision. This understanding fosters transparency, promotes effective communication, and helps avoid conflicts, ultimately leading to a harmonious financial partnership as you work together to achieve your shared financial aspirations.

Identify Shared and Individual Financial Goals

In the process of setting joint investment goals, it's crucial to list both shared and individual financial objectives. Identifying common goals helps create a strong foundation for your joint investments, allowing you to allocate resources and work as a team toward achieving these milestones.

Additionally, acknowledging individual ambitions is equally important, as it ensures that each partner can pursue personal financial dreams while respecting the partnership's financial priorities. This balance of shared and personal goals allows for clear expectations and open communication, ultimately leading to a comprehensive investment strategy that caters to both your collective vision and individual aspirations. It forms the basis for a harmonious and fulfilling financial partnership where all financial objectives, whether mutual or personal, are valued and considered.

Explore Financial Products with Mutual Advantages

Exploring financial products that offer mutual benefits is so crucial that I've decided to break it down into sub-sections. Here's why this step is significant and how it can contribute to your successful investment strategy:

Shared Growth: Certain financial products, such as joint bank accounts, shared investment accounts, or joint ownership of assets, can facilitate shared growth. These products allow you and your partner to pool resources and work towards common financial objectives. They are particularly useful for goals like saving for a down payment on a home, funding a family vacation, or building a joint emergency fund.

Income Generation: Some investments and financial instruments, like dividend-paying stocks, mutual funds, or real estate investments, can provide regular income. Exploring such products can be valuable if your joint investment goals involve creating a stream of income, whether for daily expenses, retirement, or specific financial milestones.

Risk Management: When setting investment goals as a couple, it's essential to consider risk management. Diversifying your investment portfolio with products like mutual funds or exchange-traded funds (ETFs) can help spread risk across various asset classes. This approach can protect your investments from market volatility and is particularly crucial for long-term goals like retirement planning.

Tax Efficiency: Many financial products offer tax advantages, such as retirement accounts. Utilizing tax-efficient investment vehicles can enhance your joint investment strategy by minimizing tax liabilities and allowing your investments to grow more effectively.

Estate Planning: If your investment goals extend to estate planning, products like joint tenancy with rights of survivorship can be essential. These ensure a smooth transfer of assets to the surviving partner, simplifying inheritance matters and protecting your combined financial legacy.

Liquidity Needs: Depending on your investment objectives, consider the liquidity needs associated with various financial products. Some investments, like fixed-term certificates of deposit (CDs), lock in your funds for a set period, while others, like money market accounts, offer more immediate access to cash.

Understanding these distinctions is vital for matching the product to your specific goals.

Professional Guidance: When exploring financial products, seeking advice from a financial advisor can be beneficial. They can help you select products that align with your investment goals, risk tolerance, and time horizon, ensuring that you make informed decisions.

Exploring financial products with mutual advantages allows you to tailor your investment strategy to your specific goals and risk preferences. This step is instrumental in ensuring that your investments align with your joint vision and contribute to your financial success as a couple.

Maintain a Clear Focus on Your Ultimate Objectives

Maintaining a clear focus on your ultimate financial objectives is crucial when setting joint investment goals as a couple. This focus ensures that both partners are aligned with the intended outcomes, reducing the likelihood of misunderstandings and disagreements. It serves as a source of motivation, particularly during challenging times or market fluctuations, by reminding you of the rewards and financial security you're working toward.

Regularly revisiting your end goals enables you to monitor your progress, make necessary adjustments, and celebrate milestones along the way. Additionally, it promotes open communication, adaptability to changing circumstances, and mutual accountability within the partnership. By keeping your end goals in sight, you can work together effectively to turn your shared vision into a financial reality.

Common Investment Options for Couples

Investing as a couple offers a wide array of possibilities, and there's no one-size-fits-all solution. Just as every couple is unique, the investment options available are equally diverse. Different couples have different financial goals, risk tolerances, and preferences. In this section, we'll explore some common investment options that couples often consider (Ponaka, 2023):

Medical Insurance

Being prepared for unexpected life events is crucial. Adequate insurance plays a key role in safeguarding your hard-earned money. Life insurance ensures that, even after your passing, your family won't face financial difficulties. In today's world of skyrocketing healthcare costs, health insurance is equally vital. Without it, medical expenses could quickly deplete your savings. To secure your family or partnership's financial well-being in a health emergency, your insurance plan should cover hospital admissions and related medical and diagnostic expenses.

Home Loan

Many of us aspire to own our dream home, be it an independent villa or a stylish apartment. Home loans for couples are readily available; however, taking on a loan, especially one that extends for a decade or more, can be a financial commitment that comes with uncertainties. Unforeseen events, such as job loss or the unfortunate passing of the primary earner, can make repaying the loan difficult.

In such situations, opting for a joint home loan is a prudent choice. It provides financial security as both spouses' incomes act as a cushion during unexpected setbacks. In addition to this, there are tax benefits associated with joint home loans. Each spouse can claim deductions for interest payments.

Emergency Fund

Life can be full of unexpected financial challenges, such as sudden job loss, urgent medical expenses for a family member, or unforeseen crises. Maintaining an emergency fund is essential to safeguard your financial well-being during these unpredictable times. This fund serves as a financial safety net, providing peace of mind and protection against unexpected setbacks.

The question of how much to invest in an emergency fund doesn't have a one-size-fits-all answer, as it depends on individual circumstances. However, a general guideline is to set aside an amount equivalent to 6 to 8 months' worth of your salary (Ponaka, 2023). Family needs and income sources may vary from one household to another, making it even more crucial to have a partner who can collaborate in building this financial buffer. This collaborative effort allows you to save more effectively and create a secure foundation for your future.

Mutual Funds

In the realm of investment opportunities, there's an abundance to choose from. However, among the myriad options, mutual funds shine as one of the most attractive investment vehicles. Fund houses offer the flexibility for investors to jointly hold their investments, accommodating a maximum of three holders. This feature is a valuable asset for you and your partner, as it allows for collaborative investment planning.

Investing in mutual funds can be executed through either lump-sum investments or systematic investment plans (SIPs). Opting for regular investments at a young age can yield remarkable results over the long run. Platforms like Scripbox can be immensely helpful by recommending the best funds tailored to your specific profile and risk appetite (Ponaka, 2023).

As you envision significant financial milestones, remember that one of the advantages of being in a relationship is that you don't have to embark on this journey alone. Involve your partner as an active investor alongside you. Transition your financial planning into a mutual effort rather than relying solely on one person's decisions. With an additional perspective in your financial planning, you're more than likely to make wiser choices.

Section 3: Retirement Goals and Saving Strategies

Any smart couple knows they should prepare for the future, especially when they envision their relationship lasting long-term. Retirement is a major milestone that requires careful consideration and planning. It's a phase of life when you want to enjoy the fruits of your labor and spend quality time together.

In this section, we'll explore retirement goals and saving strategies tailored for couples looking ahead to their golden years. Whether you're early in your journey or approaching retirement, understanding the steps to secure your financial future together is essential. So, let's delve into the world of retirement planning and ensure you're well-prepared for the days when you can sit back, relax, and cherish your time as a couple.

Why You Need Retirement Planning

Couples need a retirement plan for various compelling reasons. Here are some of the key factors that emphasize the importance of retirement planning:

Financial Security: Retirement often means a significant reduction in regular income or even its cessation. With a well-structured retirement plan, couples can maintain their financial stability and enjoy their post-working years without constantly worrying about money.

Quality Time Together: Retirement offers the opportunity for couples to spend more quality time together. This can involve traveling, pursuing hobbies, and simply enjoying each other's company without the constraints of a work schedule.

Healthcare Expenses: As people age, you can expect healthcare costs to rise. A good retirement plan ensures that you're financially equipped to handle medical expenses without compromising your quality of life.

Legacy and Inheritance: Couples often want to leave behind an estate or inheritance for their loved ones. Retirement planning helps structure your finances so that you can pass on your assets efficiently and minimize tax implications.

Peace of Mind: Knowing that you've prepared for your retirement can provide peace of mind. It reduces stress about the future and allows you to fully embrace this new phase in your life.

Travel and Experiences: Many couples have dreams of traveling during their retirement. With a financial plan in place, you can explore new destinations, cultures, and experiences without hesitation.

Changing Lifestyle: Retirement might bring about lifestyle changes. Whether it's downsizing your home, relocating to a different area, or pursuing new interests, a well-thought-out retirement plan can accommodate these transitions.

Unexpected Expenses: Life is unpredictable, and unforeseen expenses can arise. A retirement plan acts as a safety net, ensuring you're financially prepared for unforeseen situations, such as home repairs or family emergencies.

Longevity: People are living longer, and planning for a longer retirement is crucial. Your savings need to last so you don't outlive your resources.

Social Engagement: Having a financial plan allows you to stay socially engaged during retirement. You can join clubs, participate in community activities, and maintain an active social life.

In summary, a retirement plan isn't just about securing your finances; it's about ensuring a fulfilling, comfortable, and enjoyable life as a couple during your later-in-life years. It's a roadmap that helps you achieve your retirement goals and make the most of this special phase in your life.

Understanding each other's retirement expectations

Understanding each other's retirement plans before integrating them is crucial for a harmonious and secure future together. By doing so, you can:

Align Your Goals: Everyone has unique aspirations for retirement. One partner might dream of traveling the world, while the other envisions a quiet life in the countryside. Understanding these individual dreams is essential to finding common ground and aligning your goals for retirement.

Ensure Financial Compatibility: Assessing each other's financial standing and goals helps ensure that your plans are financially compatible. You can identify disparities and address them before they become conflicts, ensuring that your retirement plans complement each other.

Plan Together: Retirement planning is a collaborative effort. By sharing your goals and discussing your vision for retirement, you can work together to create a joint plan that accommodates both partners' needs and desires.

Avoid Surprises: Misalignment in retirement plans can lead to unpleasant surprises down the road. Understanding your partner's expectations and financial situation enables both of you to make informed decisions and avoid potential misunderstandings in the future.

Plan for Contingencies: Life is unpredictable. By integrating your retirement plans, you can consider contingencies, such as health issues, caregiving responsibilities, or changes in income, and incorporate them into your joint retirement strategy.

Optimize Resources: Integrating retirement plans allows you to maximize your collective resources. You can explore investment opportunities, tax strategies, and other financial benefits that might not be apparent when planning separately.

In conclusion, understanding each other's retirement plans is a foundational step for couples. It enables you to build a future that is both personally fulfilling and financially secure. By aligning your goals, planning together, and accommodating each other's dreams and aspirations, you can create a shared vision of retirement that strengthens your relationship and provides peace of mind for the years ahead.

Determining Joint Retirement Savings Targets and Strategies

Preparing for an unknown future, especially one in your 70s or 80s, can indeed be a challenging task. Setting money aside for a period when you're still quite far from experiencing it can be daunting. However, planning for retirement is a necessary step in securing your financial future. To make this process less intimidating and more manageable, consider these helpful tips:

Start Early: The earlier you begin saving for retirement, the better. The power of compounding interest allows your money to grow over time, helping you accumulate the wealth you need to support a comfortable retirement.

Define Your Goals: Take some time to envision your retirement lifestyle. Consider where you want to live, what activities you'd like to pursue, and any specific goals you have in mind. These objectives will provide a clear roadmap for your savings plan.

Budget and Save: Establish a budget that includes regular contributions to your retirement accounts. Setting up automatic transfers to these accounts can make savings effortless.

Diversify Your Investments: Diversification is a key strategy to help manage risk in your portfolio. Spread your investments across different asset classes, such as stocks, bonds, and real estate, to mitigate potential losses.

Monitor and Adjust: Regularly review your retirement plan and make necessary adjustments as your life circumstances change. This could include changes in your financial situation, goals, or risk tolerance.

Take Advantage of Retirement Accounts: Maximize contributions to retirement accounts such as 401(k)s or IRAs. These accounts offer tax advantages that can help your savings grow more efficiently.

Seek Professional Advice: Consult a financial advisor or planner to create a tailored retirement strategy. They can offer valuable insights and guidance to help you achieve your goals.

Remember, preparing for retirement is a gradual process, and staying consistent and adaptable to changing circumstances is key. While the future may seem uncertain now, thoughtful planning and prudent financial decisions can help you approach retirement with confidence.

Moreover, The Ultimate Retirement Planning Guide for 2022 shared the following helpful pointers to factor into your calculations when figuring out how much you and your partner need for retirement (Borzykowski, 2022):

Consider:

- **Housing Costs:** This encompasses expenses related to your place of residence, such as rent or mortgage payments, utility bills (heating, water), and maintenance costs.

- **Healthcare Costs:** Health expenses during retirement can be significant. Estimates suggest that an average couple may require around $295,000 in today's dollars for medical needs in retirement, excluding long-term care.

- **Day-to-Day Living:** Basic living expenses, including food, clothing, and transportation, need to be factored into your retirement budget.

- **Entertainment:** Your retirement should be enjoyable, so budgeting for entertainment, such as dining out, movies, and cultural activities like theater or festivals, is essential.

- **Travel**: Many retirees look forward to traveling in their post-working years. Budget for flights, hotels, and transportation costs if you plan to explore new destinations.

- **Possible Life Insurance:** Depending on your situation, life insurance may still be a part of your financial planning.

There isn't a one-size-fits-all answer when it comes to the ideal savings amount for retirement. The figure you need to save can vary based on your desired lifestyle, location, health, and personal goals. While experts often suggest savings goals like $1 million or $2 million, it's essential to remember that these are general guidelines. Your unique circumstances and preferences should be the primary drivers of your retirement savings plan.

Section 4: Planning for Your Children's Educational Future

If you have children or are planning to welcome them into your life in the future, planning for their educational future is a crucial element of investing and securing their path to success. The cost of higher education has been steadily rising over the years, and it's essential to be prepared for the expenses that come with sending your children to college or university. While it might seem daunting, prudent financial planning can make this goal attainable.

The first step in preparing for your children's education is to determine the type of education you envision for them. Whether you're considering private schools, in-state public universities, or prestigious institutions, each option comes with a different price tag. You'll also need to factor in the potential inflation of educational costs. With this information, you can estimate the financial requirements for your children's education.

Once you have a rough idea of the costs, it's time to create a dedicated savings plan. You can open a dedicated education savings account or invest in other financial instruments like mutual funds or bonds. These accounts offer specific tax advantages and are designed to help you grow your educational fund.

In addition to traditional savings plans, you may want to consider other strategies, such as scholarships, grants, part-time work during school, or co-op programs that allow students to earn while learning. As your child grows and approaches college age, you can adapt your strategy to align with their educational and financial needs.

Remember that setting aside money for your children's education is not just an investment in their future; it's an investment in your family's future. Planning wisely and starting early can provide your children with the educational opportunities they need to pursue their dreams. This financial support can significantly impact their lives, reducing their potential student loan debt and ensuring a brighter future.

Fostering Financial Romance Through Educational Planning

While financial planning and investing might not sound particularly romantic, they can indeed bring couples closer together and strengthen the bonds of a relationship. One area where this can be especially true is planning for educational investments, such as your children's college fund.

Shared Goals and Aspirations: Setting common educational goals for your children creates a sense of unity. As a couple, you can discuss the type of education you wish to provide for your children and what you want them to achieve. This shared vision not only helps in practical financial planning but also strengthens your emotional connection.

Open Communication: Discussing your children's education requires conversations about your values, aspirations, and expectations. When couples engage in these discussions and work together to achieve shared goals, it builds trust and fosters a deeper connection.

Teamwork: Planning educational investments often involves budgeting and making financial decisions together. As a team, you both play a crucial role in securing your children's future. Collaborative financial decisions can bring couples closer, demonstrating your ability to work as a unit towards a common purpose.

Shared Responsibilities: Just as you share financial responsibilities, you can also share the responsibilities of saving for your children's education. This shared commitment is not only practical but can be a beautiful expression of your love and dedication to your family's future.

Quality Time: Engaging in educational planning allows you to spend quality time together as you research and explore various savings options. It's an opportunity to learn, grow, and share experiences with your partner, further deepening your emotional connection.

Sustainable Financial Health: Planning for educational investments not only benefits your children but also your financial well-being. You're making choices now that can lead to financial stability, which, in turn, reduces financial stress and potential conflicts in the future.

In summary, educational planning can indeed be a pathway to romance within a relationship. By setting shared goals, communicating openly, working as a team, and embracing shared responsibilities, you can create a solid financial foundation while deepening your emotional connection. The act of planning for your children's educational future is a testament to your love and commitment to each other and your family's well-being.

Five Strategies for Budgeting Your Child's Education

Community Bank's recommendations on budgeting for your child's education encompass five valuable strategies as follows (December 2021):

Budgeting for Your Savings

Begin your educational savings journey with a dedicated savings account or a money market account. While the interest rates in these accounts are typically modest, they serve as an excellent starting point for housing your budgeted funds until you determine your preferred savings strategies. Numerous banks offer features like automatic transfers from your checking account to your savings account, as well as cash programs such as Pocket Change, designed to facilitate incremental additions to your savings.

Apply the "2K Rule"

Fidelity Investments introduced the 2K rule to simplify college financial planning. According to this guideline, you calculate your college savings target by multiplying your child's age by $2,000. For instance, if your child is five years old, your goal should be to have $10,000 saved for college. When your child turns 15, your target will increase to $30,000. By the time they reach 18, having saved $36,000 can significantly reduce college expenses, allowing you to bridge any remaining gap through scholarships and student loans.

Use a 529 plan or Education IRA

A 529 plan serves as a tax-advantaged savings strategy that's supported by state agencies, universities, and other institutions. This plan offers specific tax benefits, and whether or not you can benefit from these advantages depends on your state and personal situation. Using the funds for qualified educational expenses like tuition remains non-taxable at the federal level.

529 plans come in different forms, but the most common are education savings plans that operate similarly to Roth IRAs, where you invest post-tax dollars. Additionally, there's the educational savings account (ESA), which provides investment choices and an education IRA that allows tax-free withdrawals for

educational purposes. Some plans, such as prepaid tuition plans, are primarily designated for state colleges but can sometimes be converted to funds for private institutions.

Start College Early with AP Classes

One approach to trim college expenses involves reducing the number of prerequisite classes. Advanced Placement (AP) classes offer a solution by enabling students to tackle college-level coursework while in high school. If a student attains a high score on the final AP exam, they may have the opportunity to "test out" and earn credit for specific college courses, like those in English or history. This can save both time and money during their college education.

Have Your Kids Budget and Save for Their Future Education

Instill the value of saving in your children by motivating them to establish their own college savings fund. Encouraging them to have their own stake in this process fosters a sense of responsibility and underscores the importance of a college education. To further inspire them to save, consider matching their contributions with your own.

Regarding your college financial planning, explore various savings options and select those that align with your objectives. Beyond standard savings and money market accounts, you might explore certificates of deposit (CDs), which offer higher interest rates in exchange for a commitment to keep the funds untouched for a specified period, ranging from six months to a decade. You should also evaluate the advantages of investments, 529 plans, ESAs, and other savings strategies. More often than not, a combination of these methods will be most suitable.

Most importantly, commence your savings efforts as soon as possible. The earlier you start, the more you can empower your children to build a solid foundation for a successful future, culminating in a college degree.

Section 5: Managing Debt as a Couple

If you and your partner find yourselves dealing with debt, don't despair; there is a way out. In fact, many couples face financial challenges at some point in their lives, and working together to manage debt can be a crucial step towards securing your financial future as a team. This chapter delves into effective strategies for managing debt collectively, ensuring that your shared financial journey remains on a positive trajectory.

Dealing With and Avoiding Joint Debt

Joint debt isn't inherently good or bad; its implications depend on the specific couple or situation. However, what's certain is that exercising caution is paramount before embarking on the journey of co-signing a loan or jointly applying for a credit card. While love and shared plans for the future are beautiful aspects of a relationship, in these situations, applying a healthy dose of logic is even more attractive.

Before committing to any joint financial agreements, it's crucial to have a comprehensive understanding of the financial commitments involved and the potential consequences if either party fails to meet their obligations.

What Causes Joint Debt to Occur?

Do you have any questions about how joint debts work in relationships? If so, you're curious about the right things. You should walk into joint financial commitments fully aware of what you're getting into. That's because when you co-sign a loan or enter into a joint agreement like a shared credit card with your partner, you both share the legal responsibility for the debt; it's not a 50/50 split, as some might think.

Joint debts can happen with the best of intentions, especially among couples. For example, you and your spouse may decide to share a credit card to help build or improve your credit history. This shared responsibility remains the same even in situations like divorce, bankruptcy, or death. If you and your spouse decide to part ways, both of you are still equally responsible for any joint debts. So, if you co-signed a loan, credit card, or a line of credit together and one of you defaults on payments, the creditor can come after both of you, even if only one of you used the credit. In case of your partner's death, you're still obligated to pay off the remaining balance (Pangestu, n.d).

The important rule to remember is this: if your name is on the contract, you're legally responsible for repaying the debt.

What Occurs If Shared Debts Remain Unpaid?

Life can throw surprises our way, and sometimes, you find yourself facing unexpected financial challenges. One moment, you and your partner have everything figured out, and the next, you're unsure how to manage your debts. Not to frighten you, but it's wise to consider these potential situations.

When you decide to share credit, whether it's a credit card or a line of credit, it can get complicated. This can happen when, for instance, parents become responsible for their child's student loans, former spouses try to figure out shared credit card debts, or friends are left in a tight spot by someone they trusted.

When you have joint debt, both account holders are held responsible. Consequently, creditors have the legal right to demand repayment from either of you if there's any breach in how the debt should be paid. This is certainly something to think about, don't you agree?

So, if your former spouse, family member, or friend stops making payments on a loan or credit card you co-signed, you're on the hook for making those payments until the debt is fully cleared. This is why I keep emphasizing the importance of making informed decisions. If the debt remains unpaid for a while, or the co-signer defaults and time passes before the creditor contacts you for payment, your credit score will be affected.

Even if you have other accounts in good standing, having a joint account with late payments, or worse, a joint debt ending in bankruptcy, will harm your financial future. Apart from the extra financial burden, being a joint debtor can lower your credit score, which may affect your ability to get approved for loans in the future.

So, before agreeing to co-sign for someone or become a joint credit card holder, ponder on the responsibilities that come with it and establish whether both you and the person you're co-signing for can meet the payment commitments. If they can't, it's your credit score and money that is at stake. By thinking ahead, you can be better prepared for what might come your way (Pangestu, n.d).

Developing a Debt Repayment Strategy

Whatever circumstances may have led to a financial liability, one of the most important challenges many couples face is dealing with debt. Whether it's credit card balances, student loans, or other financial obligations, it's essential to have a plan to pay off these debts effectively. This is where the concept of "Developing a Debt Repayment Strategy" comes into play. In the following discussion, we will explore the key steps and considerations for creating a personalized strategy to tackle your debts and work toward achieving financial freedom. Whether you're facing personal debts or handling them with your partner, these pointers still apply (Landon, 2022):

The Debt Snowball

The debt snowball method operates much like building momentum while rolling a snowball across the ground. The approach is straightforward: you begin by settling your debts in ascending order, starting with the smallest ones. Create a list of your debts sorted by their balances and focus on paying off the one with the smallest balance first. Ensure that you continue making the minimum payments on all your other outstanding bills and allocate any extra funds to the smallest debt until it's entirely cleared.

This procedure is replicated for any additional debts you might have. With each balance paid off, you'll free up more financial resources to tackle the next debt in line. Furthermore, witnessing this progress can be highly motivating, helping you stay on course and watch your debts steadily disappear.

The debt snowball method is well-suited for those seeking quick and encouraging results when working towards debt elimination.

The Debt Avalanche

The debt avalanche strategy follows a comparable approach but differs in its method of organizing debts. In this approach, you arrange your debts based on their respective interest rates. To implement the debt avalanche strategy, you begin by creating a list of all your debts, listing them from the highest interest rate to the lowest. Then, your primary focus shifts to clearing the debt with the highest interest rate while ensuring that you make the minimum payments on your other debts. This approach effectively reduces the total interest payments you'll make, subsequently freeing up more money to allocate toward paying down other outstanding debts.

The debt avalanche strategy is most suitable for those who prioritize significant interest savings and are highly motivated to expedite their journey toward debt freedom.

Debt Consolidation

When juggling multiple payments and due dates becomes a challenging task, it might be worth exploring the option of debt consolidation. You can achieve this by obtaining a personal loan or a new balance-transfer credit card.

With debt consolidation, a lender settles all your existing debts and combines them into a single, new loan that requires just one payment. While the new loan's interest rate may be higher than that of some of your previous debts, it can lead to potential savings by avoiding missed or late payment fees.

To determine if this strategy aligns with your financial situation, you'll want to calculate your blended interest rate. This is the collective interest rate applied to all your debts. You can calculate it by adding up the total interest you're expected to pay over a year and then dividing it by the entire principal owed. Alternatively, you can make use of a debt consolidation calculator.

Even if the interest rate on a debt consolidation loan appears relatively high, it may still be lower than the blended interest rate you're currently dealing with. In such a scenario, opting for a debt consolidation loan could be a wise choice.

Debt consolidation is most suitable for individuals who can commit to refraining from using credit cards or accumulating additional debt while diligently working to pay off their existing financial obligations.

Debt Management Plan

When you're facing a financial squeeze, turning to a debt management plan is a prudent choice. Nonprofit credit counseling organizations provide a valuable service, crafting a debt management plan tailored to your unique financial circumstances. These dedicated agencies step in on your behalf, entering negotiations with your creditors to secure various concessions. These concessions can encompass lower payment arrangements, the creation of manageable repayment schedules, and, in certain instances, the pursuit of debt forgiveness.

This approach is especially advantageous for those who grapple with meeting their minimum monthly payments. If you're searching for a strategic plan that not only lightens your financial load but also paves the way to reduced overall interest payments and a faster route to debt liberation, a debt management plan can be your answer.

Having the Debt Conversation

Starting a conversation about debt with your partner may not be easy, but it's a crucial step in maintaining a healthy financial relationship. To begin, choose a time when you both can sit down without distractions. Be open, honest, and non-judgmental. Share your own financial situation and encourage your partner to do the same.

Listen actively and ask questions to better understand each other's debts, assets, and financial goals. Together, create a plan to tackle the debt using the tips above, set a budget, and align the plan with your shared financial goals.

Remember that it's essential to work as a team. Instead of assigning blame, focus on finding solutions and supporting each other. Regularly review your financial progress and adjust your plan as needed. Building a strong financial foundation through open communication will help you manage your debt and strengthen your relationship.

♥ · $ · ♥ · $ · ♥

Just as Chapter 5 was divided into distinct sections for a smoother reading experience, the summary of this chapter will follow a similarly organized approach.

Investment Styles and Risk Tolerance:

- Make informed choices by aligning your investment styles with your financial goals and risk tolerance.

- Risk tolerance categories include conservative (low risk), moderate (balanced), and aggressive (higher risk).

- Be aware that risk tolerance can change over time, so ongoing communication with your partner is essential to adapt your investment strategies.

Joint Investment Goals:

- Collaborate on creating a budget for your shared investments, allowing you to align your financial objectives.

- Deepen your understanding of each other's investment styles, goals, and personal objectives. This helps to foster trust and open communication.

- Explore financial products that offer mutual benefits, such as growth, income generation, and risk management.

- Regularly revisiting your goals as a couple ensures that you remain on the same page and motivates you to work together effectively toward your financial aspirations.

Retirement Goals and Saving Strategies:

- Plan for a secure financial future as a couple by taking proactive steps in retirement planning.

- Prioritize understanding each other's retirement expectations to align your goals.

- Determine joint retirement savings targets and create strategies tailored to your specific financial circumstances.

- These strategies involve starting early, budgeting and saving regularly, diversifying investments, and taking advantage of retirement accounts.

Children's Education Planning:

- Plan for your children's education by acknowledging the rising costs of education and choosing a dedicated savings plan.

- Explore various strategies like education savings accounts, mutual funds, and scholarships.

- Engaging in education planning can strengthen your bond as a couple through shared goals and open communication.

- Budgeting strategies - such as starting with savings, using tax-advantaged plans, and encouraging your children to contribute - can help you achieve your educational savings goals.

Managing Debts as a Couple:

- Be cautious when dealing with joint debts, understanding the legal responsibilities and potential consequences.

- Prepare for different scenarios, including divorce or a breakup, bankruptcy, and unexpected financial challenges.

- Remember that joint debt can impact both partners' credit scores and future financial opportunities.

- Consider various debt repayment strategies like the Debt Snowball, Debt Avalanche, Debt Consolidation, or a Debt Management Plan.

- Having open and honest conversations with your partner about debt and creating a joint debt management plan will help you eliminate debt while strengthening your relationship.

That concludes Chapter 5, my friends. It was quite an extensive and enlightening read, full of valuable lessons. I invested a lot of effort in it, and I hope it provides you with valuable insights to help you manage your financial matters both in the present and in the future.

Ted and Marcus's Story

In the once harmonious home of Ted and Marcus, a storm had been brewing ever since the day Marcus came home with his belongings in a box, the casualty of a sudden round of layoffs at his company. The loss of his job struck a blow to his ego and to the couple's financial stability.

Marcus, who had always taken pride in being able to contribute to their shared dreams, now found himself adrift, his days an endless cycle of job applications and rejection emails. The more time passed, the more the weight of his unemployment seemed to grow heavier, a silent specter at their dinner table.

Ted, a dedicated nurse, worked extra shifts to help make ends meet. He adjusted their budget and reassured Marcus with unwavering support. Yet, despite his efforts to keep their spirits afloat, tensions flared over the smallest expenses.

One evening, a simple purchase—a new pair of shoes for Ted—ignited the simmering fuse. "Do you really need those now?" Marcus's voice was harsh, his question an accusation.

Ted, taken aback by his outburst, responded with a mix of hurt and frustration. "I haven't bought anything for myself in months, Marcus. Can't I—"

But he was cut off by the sight of Marcus, head in hands, his posture one of defeat rather than anger. It was then that the root of the issue revealed itself, not as a question of spending but as a reflection of Marcus's inner turmoil. His sense of inadequacy had mutated into a sharp-edged guilt that he inadvertently wielded against his partner.

It took that raw confrontation for them to peel back the layers of their distress. Marcus confessed his feelings of worthlessness and his fear that he was failing their relationship. Ted, with gentle firmness, reminded him that his value to him was not tied to a paycheck.

TED AND MARCUS'S STORY

Together, they committed to facing the challenges as a unit. They sought out community resources, career counseling, and even couples therapy to help Marcus navigate his unemployment and the emotions that came with it. Through open communication and reassurance, they not only managed to keep their financial boat steady but also learned to sail through the rough waters without turning their frustrations on each other.

CHAPTER 6

Two Hearts, One Wallet: Fostering Shared Dreams and Passion

Of course, we've all heard the horror stories of joint accounts causing financial mayhem, but guess what? It's time to flip the script and focus on the sunny side of shared finances. Not everyone's had a terrible time navigating this territory, and you know what? You can be one of those shining stars on the positive side. In Chapter 6, we're all about helping you and your partner define those shared financial dreams. Get ready to spark excitement about your future together, develop strategies to stay motivated and on track, and wave goodbye to those nagging financial disputes. It's a journey towards a future filled with unity, love, and the shared joy of pursuing your dreams. So, let's dive in and discover how to make finance a tool for building an even stronger, more passionate relationship!

Managing and Prioritizing Multiple Financial Goals

I knew a couple who were deeply in love but miles apart when it came to their financial aspirations. Sarah had a burning desire to see the world, her heart yearning for new adventures, while Mike was all about building a stable life in their hometown, investing in property, and securing their future. These opposing financial goals led to countless arguments and strained conversations about their future.

Sarah's wanderlust took her to far-flung destinations, but she could still feel Mike's silent disapproval. Each adventure only seemed to deepen the chasm between them. It wasn't until a heartfelt conversation that they decided it was time to bridge their differences. They signed up for an online course on personal finance that they could complete together, increasing their financial literacy and supporting each other through the learning process.

The course encouraged them to think about the bigger picture, and they realized that both travel and property investments could fit into their lives. They crafted a plan where they could compromise and achieve a balance between adventure and stability. Sarah agreed to prioritize saving for travel but within a budget, while Mike agreed to invest in property, but they would still reserve time and funds for the occasional adventure.

Over time, the couple discovered that their joint dreams of financial security and exploration could coexist. By discussing their financial goals openly and finding a middle ground, Sarah and Mike managed to repair their relationship and, ultimately, find one harmonious voice for their financial future.

Now, many couples might relate to this in their own unique way. However, more often than not, an honest conversation and a willingness to compromise on both ends can really go a long way. Merrill Financial Bank of Africa had the following insights to share on how to juggle competing financial goals (2023):

1. Consider Your Values and Goals

On a nice and relaxed day when both of you have no pressing obligations that could cloud your judgment, sit down over your preferred beverage and make a list of words and expressions that reflect your shared values and what truly matters to you both.

According to Galinskaya (The managing director and head of the Merrill Center for Family Wealth), once this is done, you can distill these values into concise statements, ideally no more than a sentence or two in length (Merrill Financial

Bank of Africa, 2023). These statements will serve as guiding principles for your family or partnership's financial choices. For instance, if you both care about giving back to the community, this core value can influence how you allocate resources, save, and invest.

After establishing your values as a couple, the next step is to create a list of your collective goals. These goals, in turn, are molded and shaped by the values you've identified, sometimes acting as a balancing force when necessary.

Here's an example of how you might define your values and set goals based on those values:

Values Statement: Family togetherness and community involvement.

Goals:

- **Monthly volunteer work:** One of your goals could be to spend at least one day each month volunteering together as a way to strengthen your community involvement.

- **Donation**: You may decide to allocate a portion of your income towards donations to charity organizations or those in need.

- **Regular family vacations**: To uphold the value of "family togetherness," you may set a goal of taking annual family vacations to create lasting memories and bond with your loved ones.

These goals reflect your values and guide your financial decisions, ensuring that your resources are directed toward what matters most to you as a couple.

2. Sort Your List

To make headway with your financial objectives, it's essential to prioritize them effectively. You can begin by sorting each goal into one of three categories:

- **Essential Goals:** These are the non-negotiables, like building an emergency fund, preparing for retirement, and ensuring you have the financial security to cover future healthcare costs. These can't be delayed; they require immediate attention.

- **Important Goals**: This category includes objectives that hold significance to you and align with your core values. It encompasses pursuits like saving for a home, funding education, reducing debt, or leaving a meaningful legacy. While not as urgent as essential goals, they are crucial and should be given priority.

- **Aspirational Goals**: These are the "nice to have" dreams, such as owning a second home or embarking on a grand adventure. These goals, while exciting, should be at the bottom of your priority list.

By categorizing your goals as essential, important, or aspirational and distinguishing them as short-term or long-term, you can construct a deliberate plan for distributing your resources thoughtfully. This approach ensures you address immediate needs while staying aligned with your values and eventually pursuing your dreams.

3. Be On the Same Page

This tip is especially useful to couples who live with their families. It's not uncommon for couples and families who share common objectives to have varying priorities, as pointed out by Galinskaya. To help streamline your list of goals or priorities, she recommends a method known as "The First of Five." Here's how it works: when discussing a goal, each family member votes by showing zero to five fingers, indicating their level of support for that particular goal. The discussion proceeds until every goal on the list receives at least three fingers of support from everyone involved. This approach not only encourages compromise but also helps build a unanimous consensus among family members, ensuring that your financial planning aligns with the collective vision (Merrill Financial Bank of Africa, 2023).

4. Build Your Investments Around Your Priorities

With your goals in order, it's time to implement investment strategies that align with your financial aspirations. According to Galinskaya, it's wise to begin with the essential goals. Once you've established a solid plan for financing these immediate needs, you can move on to devising investment strategies for your important goals and subsequently explore avenues for your aspirational objectives.

As you build your investment portfolio, remember to take into account your risk tolerance and the time frame associated with each goal. These factors will guide your investment decisions. Additionally, consider alternative investment vehicles like a health savings account, which can assist with long-term medical expenses, or a 529 education savings account to prepare for future tuition costs.

For goals requiring near-term funding, such as purchasing a vacation home within one to three years, it's advisable to keep the money in readily accessible and secure accounts like a Certificate of Deposit (CD) or a money market account. On the other hand, for goals over five years away, like funding a child's education, consider incorporating higher risk/higher reward assets into your portfolio. When planning for goals a decade or more in the future, such as retirement, a more aggressive investment approach for growth may be suitable, allowing your investments the time and potential to recover from any market fluctuations.

5. Reconsider Your Plan Periodically

Whether it's a major shift like starting a new job or unexpected economic twists, life changes are to be expected. In such moments, it's crucial to reassess your financial plans. As Galinskaya suggests, you may need to add or remove certain goals or adjust their timelines. For instance, if you're eager to transition into a new career, even if it means delaying your retirement, consider how this choice could affect all your goals. By examining the potential ripple effect across your financial objectives, you can make well-informed decisions that don't undermine any of the things that hold significance for you.

Throughout this journey, you'll likely need to make tradeoffs. However, by following this five-step process, you'll arm yourself with the knowledge required to effectively prioritize your goals and align your resources toward realizing them. This approach ensures that your financial planning remains flexible and adaptable, accommodating the changes and surprises that life may throw your way.

Harnessing the Power of Visualization as a Couple to Transform Your Money Mindset

Money matters are not just about numbers; they are deeply intertwined with our emotions, beliefs, and attitudes. As a couple, aligning your money mindset can significantly impact your financial well-being and relationship. One powerful tool to achieve this alignment is the art of visualization.

- **Dream Together:** Start by setting aside time to dream together. Visualize your future as a couple – the life you want to lead, your aspirations, and the financial security you wish to attain. Share these dreams openly and be specific about what you see: a comfortable retirement, a dream home, traveling the world, or paying for your children's education.

- **Create a Vision Board:** Building a vision board can be an effective way to make your dreams more tangible. Gather images, quotes, and representations of your shared financial goals. Display this board in a prominent place in your home as a constant reminder of what you're working towards.

- **Practice Mindfulness:** Mindfulness meditation can help you gain control over your money mindset. It encourages you to be present, reflect on your financial choices, and become more conscious of your spending and saving habits.

- **Set Financial Affirmations:** Develop positive financial affirmations that resonate with both of you. Repeatedly affirm your shared beliefs and goals, reinforcing a money mindset that is aligned with your dreams.

- **Visualize Success:** Spend time together visualizing the steps you need to take to achieve your financial goals. Imagine the feeling of success and how it positively impacts your relationship and overall well-being.

- **Review and Adjust**: Regularly revisit your shared vision and affirmations. This practice will help you stay connected to your goals and adjust them as needed when life throws its curveballs.

By incorporating visualization into your financial journey as a couple, you can change your money mindset, align your goals, and strengthen your connection. This shared vision will empower you to work together to create a more secure financial future, fostering a strong and harmonious partnership.

Ten Tips for Staying Motivated and on Track with Your Financial Goals

Now that you've likely established your mutual financial goals as a couple and found a common vision, the question that remains is, how do you maintain the motivation needed to navigate life's twists and turns while working towards these goals? Fret not; this section is here to guide you. Here are ten valuable tips to help you stay motivated and steadfast on the path to realizing your financial dreams together. These strategies will not only keep you on course but also strengthen your bond as a couple, ensuring that your financial goals are well within reach (Jadhav, 2023):

Know the Purpose of Your Financial Goals

Understanding the "why" behind your financial objectives is essential. Take the time to delve into the deep-rooted reasons that make your goals meaningful. Knowing the purpose behind your financial goals can be a powerful source of motivation. It can be about creating a secure future for your family, having the freedom to pursue your passions, or ensuring a comfortable retirement. By clearly defining the purpose, you'll have a constant reminder of what you're working towards and why it matters.

As a couple, have open and heartfelt discussions about the underlying reasons for your goals. What will achieving these goals mean for your relationship, your family, and your individual well-being? Understanding and connecting with the purpose behind your financial aspirations can rekindle your motivation during challenging times. When the going gets tough, remembering the "why" can be the driving force that keeps you both on track and committed to your shared journey.

Incorporate this tip into your discussions and decision-making processes as a couple. Keep revisiting the purpose of your financial goals and reaffirm your commitment to them. This shared understanding will help you remain motivated and aligned as you work together to achieve your dreams.

Set SMART Goals

Ensure that your financial goals are Specific, Measurable, Achievable, Relevant, and Time-bound (SMART). Being specific about what you want to achieve, having measurable milestones, ensuring they are realistically attainable, aligning them with your values, and setting clear timeframes can provide clarity and motivation. SMART goals make it easier to track your progress and stay committed as a couple.

Break Your Long-term Goals into Small Saving Goals

Long-term financial objectives can feel overwhelming. To stay motivated, divide them into smaller, achievable savings goals. For example, if you're saving for a dream home or retirement, set monthly or yearly targets. These smaller goals provide a sense of accomplishment as you reach them and keep you motivated. Additionally, tracking your progress becomes more manageable, making it easier to stay on course. By breaking down long-term goals into smaller, bite-sized savings targets, you maintain momentum and ensure that your dreams are within reach, one step at a time.

Keep a Financial Journal and Track Your Progress

Maintaining a financial journal to track your progress can be a powerful motivator. Regularly record your financial milestones, savings achievements, and setbacks. This journal serves as a visual reminder of your journey, showcasing the progress you've made as a couple. It's a tool for reflection and rekindling your motivation when challenges arise. By seeing how far you've come, you'll be inspired to continue working towards your shared financial goals, strengthening your unity along the way.

Surround Yourself with Like-Minded People

Your social circle can significantly impact your financial motivation. Seek out friends, family members, or groups who share similar financial goals and values. Engaging with like-minded individuals offers support, encouragement, and a sense of community. You can learn from each other's experiences, celebrate successes, and navigate challenges together.

Whether discussing budgeting tips, investment strategies, or simply motivating each other to stay on track, this positive peer influence can reinforce your commitment to financial goals as a couple. Building a network of like-minded individuals provides a motivating environment that helps you both stay inspired and connected in your financial journey.

Make Your Goals Visible

Visibility is key to staying motivated. Display your financial goals prominently in your living space or workspace. This constant visual reminder reinforces your commitment and keeps your goals in focus. Whether through vision boards, goal charts, or post-it notes, having your objectives visible serves as a daily source of inspiration. As a couple, these visual cues remind both of you of what you're working toward together, reinforcing your unity and shared purpose. Making your goals visible ensures they remain a priority and propels you forward on your financial journey.

Celebrate Your Big and Small Achievements

Celebration is a powerful motivator. Make it a point to commemorate both big and small financial milestones. For smaller achievements, consider having a special home-cooked dinner, going for a leisurely walk together, or enjoying a movie night. When you reach significant milestones, like paying off a major debt or hitting a savings target, celebrate with a weekend getaway, a fancy dinner at your favorite restaurant, or a memorable experience you both cherish (as long as you stay within budget and avoid further debt). These celebrations acknowledge your progress and strengthen your bond as a couple, making the financial journey more enjoyable and motivating.

Involve Your Family in Your Financial Plan

If you have a family, including them in your financial planning is essential. Discuss your goals, share the reasons behind them, and engage your family in making decisions that impact everyone. Involving your loved ones creates a sense of shared responsibility and a support system to keep each other motivated. Your little ones can also pick up valuable financial lessons along the way. Together, you can celebrate achievements and face challenges as a united front, reinforcing the importance of your financial goals and strengthening your family's economic well-being.

Stay Prepared for the Unforeseen Challenges

Life is full of surprises, and financial plans may need to adapt. It's vital to have a contingency plan for unexpected events like job loss, medical emergencies, or economic downturns. Ensure you have an emergency fund in place to cover immediate needs. Review your insurance coverage to protect against unforeseen risks. Being financially prepared for these changes reduces stress and maintains your motivation. It allows you to navigate disruptions without derailing your long-term financial goals. As a couple, discussing and planning for the unexpected ensures you remain resilient and committed to your financial journey, no matter what life throws your way.

Review Your Financial Goals

Regularly revisit and reassess your financial goals as a couple. Life evolves, and your priorities may change. By reviewing your objectives, you can ensure they remain relevant and aligned with your current circumstances. This practice also allows you to track your progress, make necessary adjustments, and stay motivated. Set a schedule for these reviews, whether monthly, quarterly, or annually. When you both actively engage in this process, it reinforces your commitment to your financial journey and helps you adapt to life's ever-changing landscape while maintaining a shared vision for your future.

Financial Goals Planner and Vision Board for Couples

Creating a simple and easy-to-follow Financial Goals Planner and Vision Board for you and your partner can be done using a basic template in a document or spreadsheet software. Below is a detailed, step-by-step guide:

Step 1: Set Up Your Document

- Open a blank document or spreadsheet on your computer.

- The title is "Financial Goals Planner and Vision Board for Couples."

Step 2: Create a Table for Financial Goals

- Add a table with columns for "Financial Goal," "Priority," and "Action Steps."

- List your shared financial goals in the "Financial Goal" column.

- In the "Priority" column, rank these goals in order of importance.

- In the "Action Steps" column, jot down specific tasks needed to achieve each goal.

Step 3: Design the Vision Board

- Below the table, create a section for the vision board.

- Insert images, quotes, or symbols that represent your financial goals. You can copy and paste them from the web or use photos of your own.

- Add a caption or description for each image, explaining how it connects to your goals.

Step 4: Personalize Your Planner

- Customize the design by adding colors, fonts, or decorative elements.

- Leave space for notes, reflections, or motivational messages.

Step 5: Fill Out Your Planner and Vision Board

- Together, as a couple, start filling out the table by listing your financial goals, setting priorities, and outlining action steps.

- Complete the vision board by pasting images and descriptions that resonate with your shared goals.

Step 6: Print and Display

- Once your planner and vision board are ready, print them out.

- Display them in a place where both of you can easily see them, like your home office, kitchen, or bedroom.

Step 7: Regularly Update and Review

- Schedule periodic reviews to track your progress and update your planner and vision board as needed.

This Financial Goals Planner and Vision Board will help you both stay on the same page regarding your financial aspirations and motivate each other as you work towards achieving them.

My partner and I weren't financially aligned overnight; let me tell you, it took some effort, a couple of misunderstandings, and lots of discussions. Trials and errors were also in the mix. It was like a tango dance; we practiced until we were in sync. You, too, can get there if you're intentional.

Chapter 6 shifted our focus to fostering shared dreams and passion in managing finances as a couple. The key point here is to align your financial goals, stay motivated, and navigate life's twists and turns together. Let's review the practical tips we learned in this chapter:

- **Understand the "Why" Behind Your Goals:** Knowing the purpose of your financial objectives provides a powerful source of motivation. Delve into why these goals matter to both of you, and keep that in mind during your financial journey.

- **Establish SMART objectives:** Confirm that your financial goals are Specific, Measurable, Realistic, Relevant, and have a Time-bound component. This approach provides clarity, helps you track progress, and keeps you committed.

- **Break Long-term Goals into Smaller Steps:** Divide long-term goals into smaller, achievable targets. This approach offers a sense of accomplishment and makes tracking progress easier.

- **Keep a Financial Journal:** Maintain a financial journal to record milestones, achievements, and setbacks. It serves as a visual reminder of your progress and helps rekindle motivation during challenges.

- **Surround Yourself with Like-Minded People**: Seek out friends, family, or groups who share similar financial goals and values for support and encouragement.

- **Make Your Goals Visible:** Display your financial goals prominently in your living or workspace to keep them in focus as a daily source of inspiration.

- **Celebrate Achievements:** Commemorate both big and small milestones with special activities, reinforcing progress and strengthening your bond.

- **Involve Your Family:** If you have a family, include them in your financial planning to create a sense of shared responsibility and support.

- **Be Prepared for the Unforeseen:** Life brings surprises; having an emergency fund and robust insurance coverage ensures you can adapt to unexpected challenges without derailing your goals.

- **Regularly Review Your Goals:** Revisit and reassess your financial objectives as a couple to ensure they remain relevant and aligned with your current circumstances.

Set a time to create a Financial Goals Planner and Vision Board to visualize and plan your shared financial journey. This tool helps you stay on the same page and motivates both partners to work towards your financial dreams.

Maya and Leo's Story

Meet Maya and Leo, a couple who believed that a strong relationship was built on open communication, especially about topics as sensitive as finances. Every first Friday of the month, they dedicated the evening to what they playfully called "Financial Date Night."

One such evening, they settled into their cozy living room, a spread of Leo's homemade pasta and Maya's famous chocolate brownies between them, the ambient light of candles flickering softly. Their phones were turned off, and their financial documents were neatly arrayed on the coffee table.

They began with a toast to their goals, acknowledging both their progress and their challenges. With each bite and each discussion point, they reviewed their budget, celebrated the targets they'd met, and strategized on how to approach their upcoming expenses and investments. Maya would outline the benefits of diversifying their portfolio, while Leo would crunch numbers, showing potential outcomes.

Laughter and serious contemplation intermingled as they discussed dreams of future travels, a bigger home, or starting a family, all grounded in the reality of their financial capabilities and plans. The rule was simple: no blame, no shame, just a shared journey towards financial understanding and health.

As the night wound down, they updated their joint spreadsheet, a satisfying symbol of their teamwork. With each Financial Date Night, Maya and Leo not only strengthened their financial foundation but also their trust and partnership, turning what many couples find stressful into an evening of connection and collaborative planning.

♥ · $ · ♥ · $ · ♥

Chapter 7

Teamwork Makes the Dream Work: Structuring Monthly Finances and Division of Responsibilities

This chapter provides a few more detail-level insights into managing finances as an in-sync couple. It's like a dynamic duo – Batman and Robin, Bonnie and Clyde (minus the illegal activities, of course) – tackling the practical side of monetary life together. Ever wondered how to seamlessly handle your joint accounts? Who's going to be the Batman in charge of bill payments, and who'll play Robin keeping tabs on expenses? Well, this chapter has your back.

Are you a spreadsheet expert who loves to crunch numbers or a partner with a talent for strategic planning? Maybe one of you is the "money-saving ninja," while the other is the "investment guru." What strengths do you bring to your financial partnership?

We'll explore how to allocate responsibilities, set up a budget that doesn't feel like a straitjacket, and employ tools for efficient expense tracking. Think of it as the Batcave of your financial superhero journey – equipped with financial planning gadgets and a clear division of responsibilities.

And hey, don't forget, even Batman and Robin had their quirks. What are your financial quirks as a couple? Are you both meticulous savers, and does one of you tend to splurge on bat gadgets (metaphorically speaking, of course)? We'll discuss how to embrace these quirks and turn them into financial superpowers.

So, suit up (or, rather, pencil up) as we embark on this financial adventure. By the end of this chapter, you'll be ready to leave those budgeting battles behind and conquer the financial world as a dynamic duo.

The Pros and Cons of Combining Finances as a Couple

In this section, we delve into the pros and cons of combining finances; we've touched on this topic in earlier sections, but it's crucial to emphasize why you should or shouldn't take the leap into the world of joint finances. It's not about making a decision based solely on butterflies and dreams; it's about making an informed choice that suits your unique partnership. Let's dive in (Hayes, n.d):

Pros:

Most couples have individual debts, assets, and accounts, making merging accounts challenging. However, some factors can make that decision worthwhile, including the following:

Greater Security for Women

Despite recent advancements, there is still a gender gap in pay between men and women; in addition, women are more prone to income interruptions, especially when they take time off for maternity and family-related responsibilities. This leads to many women viewing combining finances as a way to ensure more financial stability. In fact, studies indicate that women experience increased financial security when they merge their finances with their spouses or partners (Hayes, n.d). While this may appear counterintuitive, many women would agree with this.

Simplicity

Dividing finances might be viable for certain couples, but it can also introduce complex discussions. Questions may arise about bill payments, how to handle income disparities, and who should cover expenses during date nights. When all the income is pooled and expenses are managed from a joint account, it can streamline these matters and make financial management more straightforward.

Flexibility

Having a partner who can financially support you when you need to take parental leave, pursue higher education, or launch a new business can boost your confidence in taking career risks. In the long term, these risks can benefit both individuals in a relationship if they lead to success. Conversely, if you're still responsible for your financial commitments during such life-changing endeavors, it might deter you from taking that bold leap.

Fosters Common Objectives

We all desire to share common ground with our significant other; when all the finances flow from a single source, it necessitates united communication. This shared financial structure can be quite advantageous, as it encourages couples to cultivate mutual financial aspirations and collaborate toward achieving them.

Cons:

It's good to know the flip side of something to make an informed decision and not be caught by surprise when things don't go your way. As with everything else in life, combining finances with your partner comes with its fair share of issues. Here are some of the most noteworthy ones (Hayes, 2017):

Amplifying the Significance of Debt

If one partner enters the union with substantial financial challenges, such as significant debt or a poor credit history, it can strain the relationship. In such cases, it might be more prudent to maintain separate accounts while the person dealing with debt takes steps to improve their financial situation. This approach can lead to a healthier financial foundation for both of you and promote a more harmonious relationship.

You May End Up Feeling Constrained

I personally value the freedom to spend my income as I see fit. While this may not apply to everyone, I appreciate the ability to make choices about my expenses without always having to discuss them with my partner first. Don't get me wrong; collaboration is essential, but a little personal financial freedom goes a long way. As adults, it's natural to want autonomy over our spending, considering that we've worked hard to earn it. However, when all finances are combined, you may find yourself in a situation where your partner has a say in your spending decisions, which can be a significant adjustment.

May Lead to Disagreements

What if each partner holds a distinct perspective on financial responsibility? Perhaps one prefers prioritizing mortgage payments, while the other believes in prudent investments. One partner may be more frugal, while the other tends to spend more freely. In such scenarios, merging finances demands open and earnest communication, along with a willingness to find a middle ground through compromise.

How to Keep Things Separate

Now that you know the pros and cons of merging finances, if you choose to keep your financial matters separate, there are several ways to approach it. Maintaining individual financial accounts while sharing expenses can be a suitable option for many couples. This strategy allows each partner to retain financial independence while still managing shared responsibilities. Here's how:

- **Split Shared Expenses:** Divide essential expenses, such as rent or mortgage, utilities, groceries, and other bills, so that both partners contribute proportionally to their incomes. (Keep reading to learn exactly how to do this.)

- **Joint Account for Shared Expenses:** Open a joint account exclusively for shared expenses. Both partners can contribute a predetermined amount to cover these costs, ensuring financial transparency and shared responsibility.

- **Individual Savings and Investment Accounts:** Maintain your personal savings and investment accounts to cater to your individual financial goals. This way, you can manage your long-term financial plans independently.

- **Clear Communication:** Ensure open and transparent communication about your financial arrangements. Discuss how you'll handle shared expenses and potential financial goals or commitments as a couple.

- **Regular Financial Check-Ins:** Plan periodic financial check-ins to discuss the division of expenses and to ensure that both partners are comfortable with the arrangement.

- **Emergency Fund:** Consider building a joint emergency fund to cover unexpected expenses that may arise.

Remember, the key to success in maintaining separate finances while in a partnership is communication, trust, and a mutual understanding of your financial goals and responsibilities. By establishing a well-defined financial structure, you can navigate the complexities of managing finances independently while still enjoying the benefits of a shared life.

Advantages of Maintaining Individual Finances

Numerous methods can be employed to maintain separate finances as a couple (as we've just learned above). Likewise, there are different approaches to take, like opting for an equal split of expenses, basing the division on income disparities, or having a joint account for shared expenses like housing while maintaining individual accounts for other financial matters. Regardless of the approach you adopt, there are several compelling reasons to consider the path of separate finances (Hayes, n.d):

Avoiding Involvement in Each Other's Financial Issues

If at all possible, my advice is to handle your financial problems independently without involving your partner. While some assistance may be necessary, expecting them to split financial debt equally may be perceived as unfair by many. Ensure transparency throughout the process, and make an effort to resolve your financial challenges on your own before turning to your partner for help.

More Autonomy for Both of You

We all have our unique goals, dreams, and personal indulgences. There's a distinction between spontaneous spending and rewarding yourself for your hard work and achievements. It's appealing to have the autonomy to make decisions in these areas. Maintaining control over your individual finances can potentially reduce conflicts and enable each partner to work towards their respective financial objectives more independently.

Cons:

There are also some noteworthy cons associated with keeping separate finances as a couple. Let's take a look:

It Can Diminish a Partner's Worth

Dividing household expenses based on income might appear reasonable, but it can lead to both partners feeling that their worth is directly connected to their earnings. Conversely, sharing expenses equally can create stress, particularly for a partner with a lower income.

For instance, if one spouse earns significantly more than the other and they choose to divide expenses based on income, the partner with the lower income might feel as though their financial contribution is not as substantial, which could, in turn, affect their sense of equality within the partnership. On the other hand, when both spouses share expenses equally, the one with the lower income might find it challenging to manage their share of the bills, leading to stress and financial strain.

Impact on Risk-Taking Capacity

As mentioned earlier, one of the benefits of adopting a joint financial approach is its capacity to accommodate risk-taking. With the security of your spouse's income as a fallback, you may feel more comfortable starting a business or expanding your family. However, the situation can be different for couples who split their finances unless they establish a system that allows for such ventures.

How to Fairly Allocate Financial Duties and Tasks in Your Relationship

This section will explore the art of fairly distributing financial responsibilities and tasks within your relationship. Whether you are managing shared expenses, planning for the future, or simply seeking a harmonious approach to your financial matters, finding an equitable division of duties is essential. Let's delve into strategies and insights to help you achieve a balanced and mutually beneficial approach to handling your finances together (Ramnarace, 2023):

Should You Have Joint or Separate Accounts? Try Both

Why go through the hassle of deciding between a joint or separate account when you're in a dual-income household? One straightforward approach is establishing a shared fund where both partners contribute to cover everyday expenses. Additionally, each partner can maintain individual accounts to manage their personal finances. This way, both individuals shoulder the financial responsibilities of everyday costs while preserving their financial autonomy.

According to Emily Sanders, the managing director of United Capital Financial Advisers in Atlanta, some of the most happily married couples were the ones who kept their money separate throughout their entire marriage (Ramnarace, 2023). She explained that the approach could help mitigate power dynamics and control issues often linked to financial matters within relationships.

However, a joint account demands transparency and mutual trust and reflects a shared dedication to a common objective. Sanders further suggests including both partners' names on the apartment lease or house deed. This enhances the equity within the relationship and eliminates the distinctions between "his house" and "her apartment." It becomes a shared possession, encompassing both the joys and responsibilities (Ramnarace, 2023).

What Happens If One Partner Earns More Money?

If you and your partner have significantly different income levels, you're not the only one, as this is quite common. With that in mind, I think you'd also agree that splitting expenses 50-50 isn't always the way to go (it's not always fair). Kelley Long, a member of the National CPA Financial Literacy Commission, suggests a more equitable approach based on income (Ramnarace, 2023).

To achieve this, you first list all your combined expenses, which typically include housing, taxes, insurance, and utilities. Then, consider your respective salaries. For example, if you earn $60,000 and your partner earns $40,000, you should each contribute a percentage equal to your income. In this case, you'd cover 60% of the shared expenses while your partner contributes 40%. If the rent is $1,000, you'd pay $600, and your partner would pay $400.

To ensure this method's sustainability, consider arranging direct deposits from your individual accounts into a shared joint account, each corresponding to your agreed-upon share of the expenses. It's important to review the joint account's bank statement every month, along with the incoming bills. Remember that expenses can change, such as increased cable bills or unexpectedly high gas costs. To adapt, maintain some funds in your personal accounts to cover any unforeseen overages (Ramnarace, 2023).

This approach ensures that the financial burden is shared fairly and prevents one partner from shouldering a disproportionate amount of the expenses, leading to a more balanced and harmonious financial arrangement.

Deciding Who Pays for What

When it comes to budgeting as a couple, it often starts with a simple question: What expenses do we share? Some of these are straightforward, like the mortgage, electric, and gas bills. But how do you approach individual financial responsibilities, student loan payments, the car loan you took out before your relationship began, or the balance on your credit card?

Handling these financial aspects requires open and honest communication. It's about discussing and finding solutions together. For instance, if your partner is dealing with a significant amount of debt, you might offer to assist with their payments. Alternatively, you could agree to take on a larger share of the household expenses, allowing your partner to focus on their debt obligations. On the other hand, if your partner prefers to manage their bills independently, you could take the initiative to cover discretionary or "fun" expenses from your personal account. The key is to work out an arrangement that both partners are comfortable with and that promotes financial harmony within the relationship.

Future Savings

While you and your partner may have individual goals and interests, certain savings objectives are best approached together. Part of your savings strategy should involve making joint decisions based on your shared goals. For example, you might have a short-term goal, like planning a vacation for next year, or a long-term goal of buying a house. Is your partner aware of these plans? Do they agree with you? If the answer to both these questions is no, then you may be off to a shaky start. The answer? Open communication! I can't stress this point enough: working towards the same financial objectives is crucial in order to achieve them more efficiently. It's just as important to agree on a savings amount that both of you feel comfortable with and regularly deposit that specified sum into a shared savings account every month.

Monthly Budgeting for Couples

For those who prefer the old-school pen-and-paper approach, you can use this monthly budgeting worksheet with your partner to keep your finances on track. Customize it by adding or removing sections based on your specific needs. Alternatively, I've provided a list of financial planning websites and apps with budgeting tools to help you set goals, track regular expenses, and maintain financial transparency between you and your partner.

Month/Year: [Insert Month and Year]

Household Income:

Partner 1's Income: $_____
Partner 2's Income: $_____
Other Income (if any): $_____
Total Income: $_____

Monthly Expenses:

Housing:
Mortgage/Rent: $_____
Property Taxes: $_____
Home Insurance: $_____
Utilities (Electricity, Gas, Water, etc.): $_____
Repairs and Maintenance: $_____

Transportation:
Car Payments: $_____

Fuel: $_____
Insurance: $_____
Maintenance and Repairs: $_____
Public Transportation: $_____

Food:
Groceries: $_____
Dining Out: $_____
Coffee Shops: $_____

Debts:
Credit Card 1 Minimum Payment: $_____
Credit Card 2 Minimum Payment: $_____
Student Loans: $_____
Personal Loans: $_____

Savings and Investments:
Emergency Fund: $_____
Retirement (401(k), IRA): $_____
Other Investments: $_____

Insurance:
Health Insurance: $_____
Life Insurance: $_____
Other Insurance (Auto, Home, etc.): $_____

Personal Expenses:
Clothing: $_____
Entertainment: $_____
Subscriptions (Netflix, Gym, etc.): $_____
Personal Care: $_____

Children (if applicable):
Childcare: $_____

Education: $_____
Child Support: $_____

<u>Miscellaneous:</u>
Charitable Contributions: $_____
Gifts: $_____
Miscellaneous Expenses: $_____

Total Expenses: $_____
Balance (Income - Expenses): $_____

Savings Goals:

Short-term Goals (e.g., Vacation):
Target Amount: $_____
Monthly Savings: $_____

Medium-term Goals (e.g., Home Renovation):
Target Amount: $_____
Monthly Savings: $_____

Long-term Goals (e.g., Retirement):
Target Amount: $_____
Monthly Savings: $_____

Notes:

- Fill in your respective incomes and expenses for each category.

- Adjust the budget as needed to ensure your expenses do not exceed your income.

- Discuss savings goals and allocate a portion of your income to savings and investments.

- Regularly review and update your budget together to track your financial progress.

Remember, open communication and joint decision-making are key to successfully managing your finances as a couple.

Financial planning websites and apps with budgeting tools

According to a recent survey by Javelin Strategy & Research, 41 percent of people don't use any money management app or website aside from their bank's. Are you one of this 41%? Make this simple change and instantly improve your financial trajectory.

- *Honeydue* – especially designed for couples or families to track expenses and create a joint budget – free

- *You Need a Budget (YNAB)* – simple budgeting rules to keep you on track – paid service

- *PocketGuard* – designed to help prevent overspending – free version available

- *Goodbudget* – simple and easy to use – free version available

- *Empower* – designed for budgeting and investment tracking – paid

- *Oportun* – links to your bank account and learns your spending habits – paid

- *Copilot Money* – works with multiple currencies – paid

- *Monarch Money* – integrates with outside accounts and tracks due dates – paid

- *Quicken Simplifi* – offers personalized spending plans – paid

- *Rocket Money* – prompts cancelation of unused subscriptions – paid

Chapter 7 was all about the practical aspects of managing finances as a couple. It emphasized the importance of dividing responsibilities and expenses efficiently. This chapter helped you discover your strengths in financial management and explore various methods for structuring your monthly finances. The key takeaways from this chapter are as follows:

- **The Pros and Cons of Combining Finances as a Couple:** Pros include potential greater financial security for women, simplicity in managing finances, flexibility, and promoting common financial objectives. Cons encompass the risk of amplifying the significance of debt, feelings of constraint on personal spending, and potential disagreements over financial responsibilities.

- **How to Keep Things Separate:** Maintaining individual financial accounts while sharing expenses can work well for many couples. Strategies for keeping finances separate include splitting shared expenses proportionally, having a joint account for shared expenses, maintaining individual savings and investment accounts, clear communication, and regular financial check-ins.

- **Advantages of Maintaining Individual Finances:** Keeping finances separate can help avoid involvement in each other's financial issues, provide more autonomy for both partners, and potentially reduce conflicts.

- **Cons of Maintaining Individual Finances:** It can lead to partners feeling that their worth is connected to their earnings and may impact their ability to take financial risks.

- **Deciding Who Pays for What:** Open communication is essential when deciding how to handle shared and individual expenses. Partners can support each other with specific financial obligations based on their capabilities and preferences.

- **Future Savings:** Couples should align their savings goals, regularly communicate about shared financial objectives, and agree on the amount to deposit into shared savings accounts.

- **Monthly Budgeting Worksheet for Couples:** A customizable budgeting worksheet is provided to help you keep your finances on track, facilitating the management of your monthly income and expenses.

This chapter underlined the significance of open communication, transparency, and mutual understanding when structuring your monthly finances as a couple. Whether you choose to combine your finances or keep them separate, it's crucial to make informed decisions that promote financial harmony in your relationship.

Conclusion

As we conclude our journey, let's take a moment to reflect on the transformation we've undergone. Much like money itself, our financial partnerships can be a rollercoaster of emotions, sometimes challenging, sometimes exhilarating.

There was not always financial harmony between my partner and me. It took effort, discussions, and our fair share of trial and error to reach the point we are at today. Our journey resembled a tango; we practiced until we danced in perfect harmony. The encouraging news is that, like us, you can navigate this path too. Your journey will be unique - full of twists and turns - and that's what makes it truly exciting. There's no one-size-fits-all solution in the world of finance, but one common thread unites us all—the potential to learn, grow, and improve our financial lives.

What's essential to grasp is that financial success isn't merely measured by the digits in your bank account; it's about understanding your goals, working in tandem with your partner, and cherishing the journey itself. And yes, a bit of humor can lighten the burden of budget meetings, proving that laughter is the best budget-friendly therapy.

As you embark on your own financial adventure, remember that you're not alone. You have your partner, the invaluable lessons from this book, and the power to transform your financial dreams into reality. Here's to a future overflowing with financial harmony, shared laughter during financial date night, and

CONCLUSION

a partnership that thrives. Together, you can turn your financial dreams into an exciting reality. Cheers to your financial success, and may your life be adorned with more smiles and fewer spreadsheet-induced headaches.

Thank you for joining me on this transformative journey, and I wish you and your partner all the financial happiness in the world. *The Romance of Wealth* isn't just a book; it's a guide to constructing a future brimming with financial freedom, mutual understanding, and an enduring love that only grows stronger as you continue building your financial future together.

Make a difference in 60 seconds by reviewing this book!

Your review can inspire other couples to take the first step towards financial success!

The Romance of Wealth – Personal Finance for Couples aims to empower its readers to take the reins of their finances. As you celebrate the milestones in your financial journey together, why not share your joy and learning with others? Your review of our book can be a valuable source of encouragement and guidance for couples just starting out or those facing financial hurdles. Tell us how our book helped in shaping your financial strategies and relationship goals. Your story can make a difference!

                        https://bit.ly/review4love

References

Aditya Birla Capital. (2023, February 6). *Investing as a married couple - 5 important tips to consider while investing*. Aditya Birla Sun Life Insurance. https://lifeinsurance.adityabirlacapital.com/articles/your-money/investing-tips-as-a-couple

Ancheta, A. (2022, June 26). *Investing style: meaning, examples, due diligence*. Investopedia. https://www.investopedia.com/terms/i/investmentstyle.asp#:~:text=Investing%20style%20refers%20to%20the

Anderson, T. (2022, August 3). *The do's and don'ts of combining finances with your partner*. Blog | Haven Life. https://havenlife.com/blog/combining-finances-with-your-partner/#:~:text=To%20start%2C%20leave%20some%20of

Bank, F. S. C. (2021, December 20). *5 strategies for budgeting your child's education*. Www.fscb.com. https://www.fscb.com/blog/5-strategies-to-save-for-your-childs-education

Borzykowski, B. (2022, September 20). *The ultimate retirement planning guide for 2021*. CNBC. https://www.cnbc.com/guide/retirement-planning/

Brown, E. (2021, August 27). *4 ways to resolve financial conflicts with your partner*. MoneyGeek.com. https://www.moneygeek.com/financial-planning/how-to-resolve-financial-conflicts-for-couples/

Brown, K. (2022, July 21). *7 steps for transforming your relationship with money.* Clever Girl Finance. https://www.clevergirlfinance.com/blog/transforming-your-relationship-with-money/#:~:text=Having%20a%20healthy%20relationship%20with

Cole, K. D. (2021, November 22). *What is a money script (and what's yours)? | Clarity Wealth.* Clarity Wealth Development. https://www.claritywealthdevelopment.com/what-is-a-money-script/#:~:text=%E2%80%9CMoney%20Script%E2%80%9D%20is%20a%20term

Cole, K. D. (2022, August 11). *What are the 4 types of money xcripts? | Clarity Wealth.* Clarity Wealth Development. https://www.claritywealthdevelopment.com/there-are-four-different-money-scripts-which-one-are-you/#:~:text=4%20Main%20Types%20of%20Money%20Scripts&text=Money%20Avoidance

Cruze, R. (2023, September 29). *Money and marriage: 7 tips for a healthy relationship.* Ramsey Solutions. https://www.ramseysolutions.com/relationships/the-truth-about-money-and-relationships

Davis , A. (2022, October 25). *5 healthy ways to handle money problems in your relationship.* Patient.info. https://patient.info/news-and-features/5-healthy-ways-to-handle-money-problems-in-your-relationship

Epperson, S. (2023, February 14). *Most couples are "financially incompatible," survey finds. Having a money talk could help — no matter how long you've been together.* CNBC. https://www.cnbc.com/2023/02/14/most-couples-financially-incompatible-having-a-money-talk-could-help.html

Finvision Financial Services. (2023, March 3). *How your mindset impacts your finances.* Www.linkedin.com. https://www.linkedin.com/pulse/how-your-mindset-impacts-finances-finvision-financial-services/

REFERENCES

First State Community Bank. (2021, December 20). *5 strategies for budgeting your child's education.* Www.fscb.com. https://www.fscb.com/blog/5-strategies-to-save-for-your-childs-education

Globokar, L. (2020, May 5). *The power Of visualization and how to use it.* Forbes. https://www.forbes.com/sites/lidijaglobokar/2020/03/05/the-power-of-visualization-and-how-to-use-it/?sh=6da071186497

Gourguechon, P. (2019, February 25). *The psychology of money: What you need to know to have a (relatively) fearless financial life.* Forbes. https://www.forbes.com/sites/prudygourguechon/2019/02/25/the-psychology-of-money-what-you-need-to-know-to-have-a-relatively-fearless-financial-life/?sh=157854ddfe8b

Hakeenah, N. (2021, June 2). *How fear, guilt, shame and envy sffect your financial goals.* Www.money254.Co.ke. https://www.money254.co.ke/post/money-and-emotions-how-fear-guilt-shame-and-envy-affect-your-financial-goals

Hayes, A. (2017, July 5). *Pros and cons of sharing your finances as a married couple.* USA TODAY. https://www.usatoday.com/story/money/personalfinance/2017/07/05/pros-and-cons-sharing-your-finances-married-couple/438157001/

How culture shapes our money mentality. (2021, June 18). The Financial Times. https://www.ft.com/content/8fdad5ef-ca4e-4e84-b8a0-543d24ee36c2

How much money does a couple need to retire comfortably? (2023, February 14). Thrivent.com. https://www.thrivent.com/insights/retirement-planning/ how-much-money-does-a-couple-need-to-retire-comfortably#:~:text=By%20age%2050%20%3A%20Aim%20to

Jadhav, K. (2023, April 15). *10 tips for staying motivated and on track with your financial goals.* Www.personalfn.com. https://www.personalfn.com/dwl/Financial-Planning/10-tips-for-staying-motivated-and-on-track-with-your-financial-goals

Kagan, J. (2021, November 18). *5 Key retirement-planning steps everyone should take*. Investopedia. https://www.investopedia.com/articles/retirement/11/5-steps-to-retirement-plan.asp

Landon, D. (2022, October 31). *How to pay off debt: 3 strategies and 6 tips*. Bankrate. https://www.bankrate.com/personal-finance/debt/how-to-pay-off-debt/#:~:text=First%2C%20you%20make%20a%20list

Lorz, K. (2021, May 3). *Conquer your money demons by dumping your limiting beliefs about money*. Money for the Mamas. https://www.moneyforthemamas.com/limiting-beliefs-about-money/#step-one-recognize-your-money-block-for-what-it-is

Marter, J. (2022, August 5). *How to talk about money with your partner | Psychology Today*. Www.psychologytoday.com. https://www.psychologytoday.com/us/blog/mental-wealth/202208/how-talk-about-money-your-partner

McBride, G. (2023, January 26). *What is risk tolerance, and why is it important?* Bankrate. https://www.bankrate.com/investing/what-is-risk-tolerance/

Merrill a Bank of America Company. (2023). *Managing & prioritizing multiple financial goals*. Merrill Edge. https://www.merrilledge.com/article/what-to-do-if-you-have-many-competing-financial-goals

Pangestu, D. (n.d.). *Joint debt problems: How to deal with & avoid joint debts*. Credit Counselling Society. Retrieved December 12, 2023, from https://nomoredebts.org/blog/dealing-with-debt/joint-debt-problems

Ponaka, S. (2023, November 16). *Financial planning for couple*. Scripbox. https://scripbox.com/mf/couple-goals-financial-goals/

Probasco, J. (2021, August 4). *How to rceate a budget with your spouse (in 7 steps)*. Investopedia. https://www.investopedia.com/articles/personal-finance/120315/how-create-budget-your-spouse.asp

REFERENCES

Ramnarace, C. (2023, July 18). *How should couples split finances? The complete breakdown*. HerMoney. https://hermoney.com/save/how-couples-can-split-their-money-to-be-fair/

Shubel, M. (2022, September 1). *How to overcome your limiting beliefs about money*. Clever Girl Finance. https://www.clevergirlfinance.com/blog/limiting-beliefs-about-money/

Sun, K. (2020, September 14). *Joint debt problems: How to deal with & avoid joint debts*. Credit Counselling Society. https://nomoredebts.org/blog/dealing-with-debt/joint-debt-problems

Tett, G. (2021, June 18). *How culture shapes our money mentality*. The Financial Times. https://www.ft.com/content/8fdad5ef-ca4e-4e84-b8a0-543d24ee36c2

Trantham, H. (2018, February 9). *The 3 money conversations you and your partner need to have*. NBC News; NBC News. https://www.nbcnews.com/better/business/3-money-conversations-you-your-partner-need-have-ncna846016

Twin, A. (2022, July 7). *Risk tolerance*. Investopedia. https://www.investopedia.com/terms/r/risktolerance.asp

Woods, T. (2022, August 5). *How to talk about money with your partner | Psychology Today*. Www.psychologytoday.com. https://www.psychologytoday.com/us/blog/mental-wealth/202208/how-talk-about-money-your-partner

Wooll, M. (2022a, July 19). *What are limiting beliefs*. BetterUp. https://www.betterup.com/blog/what-are-limiting-beliefs

Wooll, M. (2022b, December 16). Active Listening: What It Is and How To Improve It. Www.betterup.com. https://www.betterup.com/blog/active-listening

Printed in Great Britain
by Amazon